D0728432

THE CHRISTIAN WITNESS TO THE STATE

JOHN HOWARD YODER

Institute of Mennonite Studies Series Number 3
FAITH AND LIFE PRESS, NEWTON, KANSAS

The Institute of Mennonite Studies is
the research agency of the Associated
Mennonite Biblical Seminaries, 3003
Benham Avenue, Elkhart, Indiana.
Other publications arising out of in-
stitute research assignments have been:

Harold S. Bender, editor. *The Nature
of the Holy Life*. Scottdale, Pennsylvania: Mennonite Publishing House,
1960. 46 pp.

John H. Yoder. *The Christian and Capital Punishment*. Newton, Kansas:
Faith and Life Press, 1961. 24 pp.

Hans J. Hillerbrand. *A Bibliography of
Anabaptism,* 1520-1630. Available
through the institute, 1962. 281 pp.

Paul Peachey. *The Church in the City*.
Newton, Kansas: Faith and Life
Press, 1963. 115 pp.

2

Contents

Most of the material in this study was first prepared and brought together in 1955 as a work paper in preparation for a study conference on "The Lordship of Christ Over Church and State" held in July of that year in Puidoux, Switzerland. It was reworked as part of a study assignment given to Mr. Yoder by the Institute of Mennonite Studies in 1958-1959, with the collaboration of an advisory group to which Chester K. Lehman, Guy F. Hershberger, Esko Loewen, J. Lawrence Burkholder, Donovan E. Smucker, Jacob Enz, Howard Charles, and Gordon Kaufman were appointed. Further valuable advice and comment have since been received from Albert Meyer, J. Winfield Fretz, Elmer Neufeld, William Keeney, and Edgar Metzler.

Although the text has benefited greatly from the counsel, the position represented is that of the author alone. The text is maintained largely in the form which arose through this communal study process. This has meant gathering in the closing chapters several discussions which are not to be understood as merely technical or documentary appendixes. They deal at somewhat greater length with sample issues of background or of implementation which the main text treats only in passing. A publication subsidy from the Schowalter Foundation of Newton, Kansas, is gratefully acknowledged.

Institute of Mennonite Studies
Cornelius J. Dyck, Director
John H. Yoder, Associate Director
Elkhart, Indiana

THE CHRISTIAN WITNESS TO THE STATE

1. THE PROBLEM IDENTIFIED

THE REIGN OF CHRIST means for the state the obligation to serve God by encouraging the good and restraining evil, i.e., to serve peace, to preserve the social cohesion in which the leaven of the Gospel can build the church, and also render the old aeon more tolerable.

Thus the church's prophetic witness to the state rests on firmly fixed criteria; every act of the state may be tested according to them and God's estimation pronounced with all proper humility. The good are to be protected, the evildoers are to be restrained, and the fabric of society is to be preserved, both from revolution and from war. Thus, to be precise, the church can condemn methods of warfare which are indiscriminate in their victims and goals of warfare which go further than the localized readjustment of a tension. These things are wrong for the state, not only for the Christian. On the other hand, a police action within a society or under the United Nations cannot on the same basis be condemned on principle; the question is whether the safeguards are there to insure that it become nothing more. In practice, these principles would condemn all modern war, not on the basis of perfectionist discipleship ethics, but on the realistic basis of what the state is for.[1]

This pamphlet is fundamentally an exposition of the claim made in the paragraphs quoted above; namely, that it is possible for the Christian or the Christian church to address to the social order at large or to the state criticisms and suggestions concerning the way in which the state fulfills its responsibility for the maintenance of order.

For most Christian groups, this is a claim that needs no proving. For all of those Christian traditions whose standards and ideals concerning the church and her relation to society go back to the

---

1 J. Yoder, "Peace Without Eschatology?" (pamphlet), *Concern*, Scottdale, 1959, p. 17f.

Middle Ages it is simply assumed that, since the statesmen within a given society are probably Christian by virtue of the fact that the whole society is Christian, the ethical standards applying to the statesmen are those of the church. For all of these groups—Catholic, Lutheran, and Reformed—it is assumed, for reasons which may differ superficially but are basically the same, that all of the activities of the state, including the police function, the death penalty, and even war can be the duty and responsibility of the Christian as statesman or as soldier. This is a conclusion which nonresistant Christians are not able to accept because of their fundamental commitment of faith to Jesus Christ and the way of the cross in which He has called them to follow Him. The identification of the state's duties and the Christian's duties, from which there would follow an obligation for the Christian to serve the state in this capacity, can therefore not be admitted.

The claim stated at the outset is also self-evident and in need of no proof for the Christian pacifist position as represented by a strong popular movement within the North American churches in the 1920s and 1930s. For this position, there was no problem involved in applying Christian ethics to the state, since it was more or less assumed that it was quite possible for the state, even the modern nation, to follow the pacifist Christian's example and teaching in a simple renunciation of the use of force—or at least of military force—as an instrument of national policy. This optimism with regard to the possibility of the state's fulfilling the requirements of Christian ethics is one which neither a careful study of the Bible nor a realistic interpretation of current events can admit.[2]

If it is admitted at the same time:

a. that the Christian, by virtue of the relationship to Jesus Christ which makes him a Christian, can no longer threaten or take away the life and liberty of his fellowmen;[3] and

b. that in our society we cannot expect the social order at large to function without the use of force,

---

2 Cogent criticisms of this kind of pacifism have been presented briefly by John R. Mumaw in "Nonresistance and Pacifism" (pamphlet), Scottdale, 1944, and by Herman Hoyt, *Then Would My Servants Fight*, Winona Lake (Brethren Missionary Herald Co.), pp. 54-69. G. F. Hershberger implies some similar doubts in Chapter 9 of his *War, Peace, and Nonresistance*, 2nd ed., 1953. In a different theological world the same point is made by Franklin H. Littell in "The Inadequacy of Modern Pacifism," *Christianity and Society*, Vol. XI, No. 2; pp. 18-23 (Spring 1946). Except for verbal differences, e.g., in breadth of meanings of the word *pacifism* (usable in some contexts and misunderstood in others), the present study presupposes the basic validity of these critiques. For a more systematic treatment along similar lines cf. below p. 63.

3 This conviction, although presupposed without discussion in the present paper, will, of course, for some readers need discussion in its own right. The most adequate treatments of the theme are: Jean Lasserre, *War and the Gospel*, Scottdale, Herald Press, 1962; G. H. C. MacGregor, *The New Testament Basis of Pacifism*, Fellowship, revised edition 1953; Culbert Rutenber, *The Dagger and the Cross*, Fellowship, 1950.

it would seem to many to follow that the orientation of Christian faith as just stated leaves the Christian incapable of making any relevant contribution to the study and definition of political policy. The very nature of the state is force, and the Christian has committed himself to have no recourse to force, not only in his own interest but even for the sake of justice. Thus by far the most current interpretation of this problem in contemporary American ethical thought is that the consistent Christian pacifist must accept the verdict of political irrelevance for his position.[4] The advocacy of Gandhian nonviolent political pressure or the acceptance in certain situations of an antimilitarist national policy would be quite another matter, but the Christian who says that because of Jesus Christ or because of the law of God participation in war is excluded for him in all circumstances is thereby irrevocably cut off from the political scene. From this it need not follow that he has no value in society. Even in the political realm the awareness of the basic issue of principle which he incarnates is a necessary part of moral concern for the political order. Subject to the condition that he must not hold his position to be the *only* right one, the committed Christian pacifist has the useful symbolic function of the gadfly who constantly keeps uneasy the consciences of responsible persons as they accept the compromises necessary for effectiveness in daily political work. This symbolic "prophetic" irrelevance, this uncompromising effort at moral purity, is justified and meaningful, but only insofar as it accepts the verdict of immediate irrelevance and makes no claim to be able to suggest solutions and plan policies capable of being put into practice in the political realm.

The heritage of Christian ethical thought in our time is such that the problem as just stated must be our point of departure in the present study. Our purpose is to analyze whether it is truly the case that a Christian pacifist position rooted not in pragmatic or psychological but in Christological considerations is thereby irrelevant to the social order. Toward this end we shall, first of all, assume that the rejection of lethal violence is demanded for the Christian by the example and teaching of Christ. We shall further not attempt to argue the feasibility of establishing in our present age a kind of political or economic order somehow doing away with the need for violent action, but shall assume, for the purpose of this argument, that this is impossible. Both of these assumptions may well call for argument in their own right, but this is not the place for such argument. Within the framework of these assump-

---

4 The most coherent and convincing formulation of the current interpretation which we here summarize is to be found in many of the writings of Reinhold Niebuhr. Cf. J. Yoder, "Reinhold Niebuhr and Christian Pacifism" (pamphlet), *Concern*, Scottdale, 1959. The same general analysis may, however, also be found among thinkers who do not share all of Niebuhr's convictions on other matters.

tions and admissions we shall here attempt to ascertain on what grounds, according to what standards, and with what hope of success it is nevertheless not only possible but obligatory that the Christian should witness to the social order in a relevant way.

2. THE GROUND FOR THE WITNESS TO THE STATE

A. Christ's Lordship According to the New Testament Witness

"Jahweh says to my Lord, sit at my right hand, till I make thy enemies thy footstool."

FROM THE VERY EARLIEST record of the witness and worship of the church in the first chapters of the Book of Acts to the latest portions of the New Testament canon, the affirmation is unchanging that Jesus Christ, ascended to the right hand of God, is now exercising dominion over the world. The passage from Psalm 110 quoted above is the one section of the Old Testament most frequently cited or alluded to in the New Testament.

In order to grasp what Old and New Testament mean by this kind of statement, we need first to understand how the Bible sees human affairs to be dominated by superhuman powers, referred to biblically under many names (thrones, principalities, powers, archangels, dominions), which are often grouped by interpreters under some such heading as *angelic* or *demonic*. These powers are seen as invisibly determining human events; in biblical language *powers* would be roughly the equivalent of the modern term *structures,* by which psychological and sociological analysts refer to the dimensions of cohesiveness and purposefulness which hold together human affairs beyond the strictly personal level, especially in such realms as that of the state or certain areas of culture.[1] In short, the powers govern that realm which the Bible refers to as the

---

1 Cf. H. Berkhof, *Christ and the Powers,* Herald Press, Scottdale, 1962. Gordon Rupp (*Principalities and Powers,* Epworth, London, 1952) has well labeled this realm by listing " 'Anities and 'Alities, and 'Ologies and 'Isms . . ." (p. 15); we could add 'doms and 'hoods. Such words as *causality, fatality, necessity, humanism, respectability, Christendom, nationhood* do not point to specific people, things, or events, but neither are they mere ideas. They are realities, of a suprapersonal kind, which lend coherence to life, exercising a real power over human decision. Their impingement upon concrete events may be quite crudely visible (Fascism, sorcery) or quite imprecise and indirect (humanism, moral law). G. B. Caird (*Principalities and Powers, A Study in Pauline Theology,* Oxford, Clarendon, 1956) subsumes the meaning of the powers in four phrases (p. xi): pagan religion, pagan state power, the Jewish law, and the irrational factor in the physical universe.

world (*kosmos* in the Johannine writings, *aion houtos* according to Paul).[2]

The triumphant affirmation of the New Testament is that Jesus Christ by His cross, resurrection, ascension, and the pouring out of His Spirit, has triumphed over the powers. This is the concrete meaning of the term *Lord*. The significance of the present period of history, from Pentecost to the Parousia, is that "he must reign until he has put all his enemies under his feet" (1. Cor. 15).

The present historical period is characterized by the coexistence of two ages or aeons. The essential difference between the two aeons is not temporal, since they coexist; it is more a matter of direction. The present aeon is characterized by sin and centered on man; the coming aeon is the redemptive reality which entered history in an ultimate way in Christ. The present age, by rejecting obedience, has rejected the only possible ground for man's own well-being; the coming age is characterized by God's will being done. The seal of the possibility of His will's being done is the presence of the Holy Spirit, given to the church as a foretaste of the eventual consummation of God's kingdom. Thus, although the new aeon is described as coming, it is not only a future quantity. The old has already begun to be superseded by the new, and the focus of that victory is the body of Christ, first the man Christ Jesus, and then derivatively the fellowship of obedient believers.

The present paradoxical state of the world is well expressed in 1 Corinthians 15:20-28. Christ is now reigning, He is now Lord, yet not all His enemies have been subjected to Him. To follow the picture suggested by Cullmann, the enemies of Christ are in the situation of a warring nation whose defeat is sure because of the overwhelming forces brought to bear by the adversary, but which continues to resist for some time before the final surrender. Thus it is possible and not essentially irrational for the New Testament to tell us both that Christ has triumphed and is reigning (which is true for the church through the Holy Spirit, and for the world by anticipation) and that the powers of evil are still rampant.

It is the merit of Cullmann's work, "The Kingship of Christ and the Church in the New Testament,"[3] to have worked out most clearly this double character of Christ's reign. There is a qualitative difference between the two ways that *reign* expresses itself in the present aeon. The modern use of *kingdom of God*, a term which has commonly served to render unclear the line between church and world, is unfaithful to the biblical view in just that respect. The

---

2 We do not mean here to deny that *World* may have other meanings in New Testament or in theological usage; yet it is with reference to the rebellious creaturely order that the term seems to be used most frequently and coherently.

3 In *The Early Church; Studies in Early Christian History and Theology*, ed. A. J. B. Higgins, Westminster, 1956, pp. 105ff.

reign of the Father remains identified with the not-yet-arrived end of the age (1 Cor. 15:24); in the present period of history we have two separate anticipations of the kingdom, both of them valid foretastes of the final triumph but in different ways. The church points forward as the social manifestation of the ultimately triumphant redemptive work of God; the world, however, even though still rebellious, is brought into subjection to the kingship of Christ or the kingdom of the Son. The kingdom of the Son is thus to be distinguished, insofar as we may be permitted to speak systematically, from the kingdom of God.[4]

The mastery of God over history is not a new idea in the New Testament; the idea was current in Jewish prophetism. Isaiah 10 is a classical case to which we shall return later. It demonstrates a heathen nation being used by God for a mission of vengeance, only to fall itself under God's vengeance upon the very act of violence which God had used. Superficially the New Testament view changes this understanding of history by making it specifically Christological; the Old Testament knew that *the Lord* is the master of history; the New Testament adds that *Jesus Christ* is Lord.

But another difference is deeper. In the Old Testament it had not become fully clear, even though the beginnings of such an understanding of history were forming, just what was the meaning of the cycle of vengeance upon vengeance. The contradiction between promise and menace in the expectation of the Great Day Coming was never quite resolved in the Old Testament or in the intertestamental times. The most popular attempt at resolution was the pure and simple nationalization of the hope of Israel; the vengeance will be for the nations, the promise for Judaism; but this answer contradicted all the central insights of the true prophets. The answer could only come with the fulfillment of the prophetic hope and the clarity which the work of Christ brought to the problem of history and the divine-human community.

Jesus made it clear[5] that the nationalized hope of Israel had been a misunderstanding, and that God's true purpose was the creation of a new society, unidentifiable with any of the local, national, or ethnic solidarities of any time. This new body, the church, as aftertaste of God's loving triumph on the cross and foretaste of His ultimate loving triumph in His kingdom, has a task within history. History is the framework in which the church evangelizes, so that

---

4 1 Cor. 15:24ff; The distinction between the "Kingdom of God" and the "Kingdom of the Son" cannot be read back into the Gospel reports; before the Ascension the distinction was meaningless. Whereas the epistles recognize the temporal quality of the sitting at the right hand *until* the enemies become a footstool (especially Heb. 10:12, 1 Cor. 15:24), the citations from Psalm 110 in the Gospels do not draw any such conclusions from this phrase (Mark 12:36, 14:62, and parallels).

5 Cf. especially the chapter, "Jesus and the Resistance Movement of the Zealots" in O. Cullmann's *The State in the New Testament*, Scribners 1956.

the true meaning of history is the fact that God has chosen to use it for such a "scaffolding" service. Now the whole vengeance-upon-vengeance mechanism takes on meaning as a vehicle subordinate to the redemptive purpose; it is to maintain peace so that all men can come to the knowledge of the truth (1 Tim. 2). The interplay of violence upon violence, vengeance upon vengeance, whether in international wars such as Isaiah 10 had in mind or in the relatively more regulated processes of the state's judiciary and police machinery, has the ultimate purpose of preserving the fabric of the human community as the context within which the church's work can be carried on.

Before proceeding to analyze what the lordship of Christ means more particularly for the state, we should turn to two accessory questions which arise in the effort to relate the biblical teaching to traditional Protestant thought.

In some circles the phrase *lordship of Christ* is used quite frequently and with a meaning that is both quite definite and quite distinct from that which it has in the present paper. Over against a pietist or antinomian faith which considers Christ primarily as Saviour, this usage, current in some American free-church circles, would insist that He must also be accepted as Lord, i.e., as one to be faithfully obeyed. Thus the term *lordship of Christ* signifies not the objective status and dignity that belong to Christ by virtue of His accomplished work, but rather an honor that is ascribed to Him by virtue of some individual believers' subjective attitudes and denied Him by others. We have no quarrel with the point which this usage of the term *lord* attempts to make, namely its call for faithful discipleship. Yet the usage distorts the biblical meaning of the term by implying that Christ's lordship depends on an individual's belief.

The question may meaningfully be raised, What can *lordship* mean as long as the powers of this world are still in rebellion? Since *lord* is fundamentally a term from the realm of political authority, we can best respond to this question by pointing out that many a political sovereign, whose authority no one challenges legally, is still not effectively in total control of all the actions of all the persons and organizations in the territory over which he claims dominion and cannot force total and unconditional obedience even in realms where his sovereignty is confessed. The more traditional Protestant usage has taken the label *Providence* or *divine overruling* to designate this same divine dominion over the rebellious world. If *lordship* was discussed at all, it was with reference to the church alone. The biblical term *lordship* is different from the practically synonymous expression *providence,* not only in its being a more current political expression, but also in its more pointed relationship to Jesus Christ and its more personal and voluntaristic color.

11

B. Christ's Lordship and the State

The state—speaking now not of any one particular political pattern but of the fundamental phenomenon that society is organized by the appeal to force as ultimate authority[6]—is a deeply representative segment of the "world." In line with what has been affirmed above, this leads the New Testament church and the apostolic writers to confess that the bearers of political authority are in spite of themselves agents of the divine economy, being used whether in rebellion or submission as agents of God's purpose. When Paul notes in passing that if the "rulers of this age" had understood God's hidden wisdom "they would not have crucified the Lord of glory" (1 Cor. 2), he is affirming that the powers, meaning *both* the superhuman *and* the human agencies involved in the execution of Jesus as an insurrectionist, were in spite of themselves being used as God's instruments within a process which ultimately meant their own defeat.

Romans 13 and *1 Peter* 2 deal with the state in the most direct and affirmative way as God's instrument for the maintenance of order in society. Several of the terms in Romans 13 are derivatives of the root *taxis*, "order." The command in verse 1 might be translated "Let every soul be sub*ord*inate to the *ord*ained authorities." It is thus meaningful to speak of an "*ord*er of providence," where Christ reigns over man's disobedience, through the "powers" including the state, side by side with the "order of redemption" where Christ rules in and through the obedience of His disciples. It would be a misunderstanding to refer to one of these realms as the "order of grace," as if only the church were in the realm of grace. Both the lordship of Christ over the world and His headship in the church are of grace, though they are distinct.

The time between the ascension of Christ and the defeat of the last enemy, when the kingdom of the Son will give place to the consummated kingdom of the Father, is thus characterized by the way in which the reign of Christ channels violence, turning it against itself, so as to preserve as much as possible of the order (*taxis*) which is the pre-condition of human society and thereby also a vehicle for the work of the church. The state being, in its judicial and police functions, the major incarnation of this chan-

---

6 We here seek no doctrine of the state as divine institution, as social contract, or as leviathan. Nor are we initially concerned with the socialized welfare functions of many modern states. Numerous traditional thinkers have considered the ultimate sanction of the sword as the *essence* of the state; for others, the essence is some broader and more constructive community function but the sword remains indispensable, even if only as a "strange work" distinct from its real business. Some utopians would banish it entirely. Such debate is not our present concern, though we shall turn to it later (p. 000). Whatever the state is or should be in theory, in fact every state wields the sword, and it is that fact that sets the theme for this study. Whether some other kind of institution, which would not wield the sword and would therefore not pose all the same problems for us, should properly be called a state, is here irrelevant.

neled evil, it is perfectly logical to find the New Testament teaching on the state most clearly expressed in a context that begins by describing the transformed life of the believer (Romans 12) and ends with an evocation of the coming day (13:11 ff.) in the light of which the believer is already called to walk.

In spite of the present visible dominion of the "powers" of "this present evil age," the triumph of Christ has already guaranteed that the ultimate meaning of history will not be found in the course of earthly empires or the development of proud cultures, but in the calling together of the "chosen race, royal priesthood, holy nation," which is the church of Christ. The church is not fundamentally a source of moral stimulus to encourage the development of a better society—though a faithful church should also have this effect —it is for the sake of the church's own work that society continues to function. The meaning of history—and therefore the significance of the state—lies in the creation and the work of the church. The reason for Christian prayer in favor of the political authorities is that "God our Saviour desires all men to be saved and to come to the knowledge of the truth" (1 Tim. 2). The function of the state in maintaining an ordered society is thereby a part of the divine plan for the evangelization of the world.[7]

Careful reflection on what has been said thus far will make it clear that the New Testament thereby gives the reasons for a Christian witness to the state and the standards which would govern such a witness. Often in past history Christians have been concerned for the life and work of the state because they felt that it was itself of the most fundamental importance in achieving God's purpose in the world, whether this purpose called for the defeat of a political enemy or the establishment of a good society. Still other Christians have felt able to give moral guidance to the state simply by virtue of the fact that members of the church were at the same time responsible statesmen. In the New Testament the reason for concern with the state is different; it is that the state has within the divine plan a function, modest but nevertheless essential, constantly shifting but nevertheless fundamentally definable, distinct from that of the church yet within the redemptive plan. Although by the nature of the case the New Testament church was seldom given the opportunity to put these certainties into action (Jesus' encounter with His judges and Paul's appearance before Roman officers being almost the only cases), its understanding of the state's function is still sufficiently clear to provide the criteria for a clear

---

7 The term *evangelization* should not be conceived of too narrowly as limited to the recruiting of individual converts for the ranks of the church. Cf. below, p. 19. Yet neither may it be reduced to a generalized proclamation of social goals independent of the call to faith or of the building of the believing community.

and relevant witness to men of authority about the discharge of their functions.[8]

C. Parallel Motivations

There were good reasons to concentrate, as the above pages have done, on the New Testament's own way of interpreting the state's function. This approach makes clear that the meaningfulness of the witness to the state is not dependent on the numeric strength of the Christian population nor on the state's Christian profession or its willingness to listen. Yet there are further reasons for such concern in our day. Primary among these is certainly the very personal and very concrete concern which the Christian has for the welfare of his neighbor. The state may either threaten or further the welfare of its subjects. The more sweeping the state's claims, and the more self-conscious its manipulation of social and economic mechanisms, the more self-evident does its effect on our neighbors' welfare become. Not only does this add a dimension to our understanding of what it is that drives a Christian to testify against injustice; this consideration further reminds us that "human welfare" is in itself a value, a criterion, which, although not always abstractly definable, is usually self-evident in a given context of need. When Jesus instructed us to love our neighbors as ourselves, He did not mean to enjoin a certain measure of selfishness, either undergirding or counterbalancing our altruism; the point is much more simply that I know very well, in looking at myself, what I consider to be "good." This criterion of "human welfare" is a concept distinct from what we have been saying about the lordship of Christ; the two can, however, not be basically in opposition to one another.

Such loving concern should bind us not only to the victims of governmental injustice, but also to the statesman himself. No man can be in harmony with God or even with himself who chooses to cause others to suffer. His bondage to violence and lust for power may be brutal and frank, clouded by doubts, or cloaked in self-righteousness; it is bondage all the same. He needs neither to be fawned over or to be feared as if he were truly strong, nor to be threatened as if he were an adversary, neither to be blamed for his failures nor to be praised for his noble intentions. He needs,

---

8 It could be argued that the church's knowing of the state's place in history is not yet proof that she should speak to the statesman about it; should she not rather keep this knowledge to herself? There might be something to this if the insights or principles of which we shall speak were disincarnate truths or mysteries; but they are gospel. The putting of the powers in their place is an integral element of the work of Christ. The very fact that this is true is necessary and sufficient reason for proclaiming it to *all* men —yea, even to the powers themselves: ". . . that through the church the manifold wisdom of God might now be made known to the principalities and powers in the heavenly places" (Eph. 3:10 RSV). It can, in fact, be argued that the proclamation to the powers is not merely an *announcing* of the victory, but in fact a part of the actualization of that victory. G. C. Caird (op. cit. 84 ff.) speaks in this connection of "Victory through Revelation."

like any man, to be respected, to be esteemed worthy of personal concern, to be invited to discover—whether within his office or beyond its bounds, he can know only later—a way more excellent, more human, both for his subject and for himself. We cannot testify to human concern for the statesman as a man[9] without concern for his work.

All the more is this the case if the statesman in question is a professing Christian. According to some traditional peace church views, any involvement in the apparatus of government is reprehensible for the Christian; for others, this would apply only to directly military roles. The problem is the same in either case; there are persons taking a large or small responsibility in the political-military apparatus, the honesty and sincerity of whose confession of faith in Jesus Christ there is no *prima facie* reason to challenge. Their behavior, and presumably some of their beliefs, differ seriously from ours in ways we cannot consider justified, but this is also true of many other Christians on other issues. Here, as elsewhere, the Christian duty toward the "erring brother" is clear. "You who are endowed with the Spirit must set him right again very gently. Look to yourself, each one of you: you may be tempted too. Help one another to carry these heavy loads. . ." (Gal. 6:1, 2 NEB).

D. The Holy One of Israel

By beginning with the central New Testament proclamation and then carrying on from where current American thought had brought this problem, we have hitherto left to one side the Bible's own starting point, namely the Old Testament witness. When the prophets spoke to kings, their message was twofold:

a. *The Denunciation of Idolatry.* Whether dictated by foreign alliances and mixed marriages or by Israel's own superstition and smallness of faith, the service of alien gods was a special temptation for kings and the chief abomination of prophets. The prophets' condemnation was called down not upon moral misbehavior but upon spiritual disloyalty; not on misdeeds but on idolatry. Today such idolatry can dispense with the ethereal deities of Babylonian faith and with the earthy ones of Canaan, for the nation itself has taken on the worship claims of both. War, to cite but one case, does not first become wrong when the missiles are sent off; the prior choice of nationalism, preferring one people, one state absolutely above all others, is already idolatry. Nationalism sins against the first two commandments well before it infringes on the second table of the law. Not only in the crude forms of Fascism and Nazism is nationalism idolatry; the same idolatrous claim is already made

---

9 Cf. below p. 21.

for a created value when it is thought that a given civilization or nation is the bearer of the meaning of history; when a given nation, like the United States in the Cuba crisis, claims the right to be judge, jury, and executioner in its own case.

b. *God's Working with Israel.* Having created the nations and assigned to each of them its place and destiny, Jehovah, according to the prophets, continued to be concerned about their doings not so much for their own sake as for the sake of Israel. Sometimes the work of the princes is to bless Israel (especially Cyrus, Isaiah 40 ff.); oftener to chastise (Isaiah 10). Israel's only duty is to accept these providential workings, to renounce other means of defense (Isaiah 30, 31), to accept even captivity (Jeremiah 21), and to learn through these events that stillness in which there is strength.

Although some prophecies are addressed literally to pagan princes (Isaiah 45, Amos 1, 2), there is doubt of their having been delivered to the addressees. We thus have here a precedent for interpreting the meaning of political events, but not for speaking to statesmen. But insofar as the western world seeks to keep wearing the cloak of Christendom, the reminder that God *chastens* His people through history is well raised. If in the Cuba or Berlin crisis we had thought first to ask what these events meant for the purging and the redeeming of the church, the light in which we had then spoken to the authorities might have changed notably.

3. THE FORM OF THE CHURCH'S WITNESS

A. *The Church's Existence as a Witness*

THE ABOVE DISCUSSION should have made it clear that the Christian church knows why the state exists—knows, in fact, better than the state itself—and that this understanding provides both the justification for her speaking and the standards which she will apply in evaluating the way in which the authorities exercise their function. Before proceeding to a more careful logical analysis of the standards she will use and the way she will apply and communicate them, we shall seek to survey the several dimensions of this witness as functions of the life of the church.

The first level of the church's faithfulness, and in a sense the test of the validity of everything else she shall say later, will be her own obedience to the standards of discipleship. If it is clear to the church, as it was in New Testament times, that the central meaning

16

of history is borne not by kings and empires but by the church herself, then her first duty to society will be the same as her first duty to her Lord. Her witness to the primacy of her faith will be visible in evangelistic activity (in the traditional, restricted sense of that term, a usage itself open to challenge), but just as fundamentally in the service of the needy, and equally in her refusal to use means unfitting to her ends. What we say here of the church is valid for the individual Christian as well. He will not permit his local obligations to one particular state to lead him to treat in an unbrotherly way an enemy of that state. An attempt, for example, to justify war for the individual Christian citizen, after it has been judged incompatible with the ministry of the church, is a refusal to be honest with the absolute priority of church over state in the plan of God.[1]

The church is herself a society. Her very existence, the fraternal relations of her members, their ways of dealing with their differences and their needs are, or rather should be, a demonstration of what love means in social relations. This demonstration cannot be transposed directly into non-Christian society, for in the church it functions only on the basis of repentance and faith; yet by analogy certain of its aspects may be instructive as stimuli to the conscience of society. For the church and the reign of Christ will one day be englobed in the same kingdom. That kingdom will mean the victory of the church and the overcoming of the world; as anticipation of that consummation it is possible for the potentially victorious order to testify to the potentially vanquished order concerning the absolute norm which is valid for both and in contradiction to which the world will never succeed in building even a stable temporal order. It is an expression of the social character of the church that Jesus' proclamation of the kingdom, while not political in the sense of the Zealot aspirations, was still political enough to be misunderstood by the Zealots, by some Jews, and by Pilate as being of the same nature. Paul testifies to a sort of social self-sufficiency and at the same time gives us a pointed commentary on the teaching of Romans 13, when in 1 Corinthians 6 he directs Christians to have their own judicial processes within the church, and to accept innocent suffering rather than to submit their disputes to the governmental tribunals, variously designated as "unrighteous," "those who are least esteemed by the church," and "unbelievers."

In modern usage the application of the term *political* to the state rather than to the church is so well established that it cannot

---

1 It should be clear that this "priority of church over state" has nothing to do with clericalism, in which the organized church herself adopts the standards of the state, views herself sociologically and not theologically, and accepts for herself the secular conviction that the meaning of history is to be found in politics.

be combatted. It leads to a distortion, however, for in biblical thought the church is properly a political entity, a *polis*. In both biblical languages the word *church* (*qahal, ekklesia*) refers originally to a deliberative assembly of the body politic. Though the disparagement of the cultic and the priestly elements in the old covenant has gone too far in some recent theology, it does remain true that biblical language about Christ and the church is more political (kingdom, Messiah, New Jerusalem, *politeuma*) than cultic. In this root sense, therefore, the church is more truly political, i.e., a truer, more properly ordered community, than is the state.[2]

One of the significant points at which the inner life of the Christian congregation can provide stimulation and insights to the larger community is the biblical understanding of the diversity of ministries, or the sharing of responsibilities within the Christian fellowship. Over against the tendency toward hierarchical structures of authority in pagan society, there is within the Christian church an egalitarian thrust which casts light beyond the borders of the church. The church does not begin directly by attacking the social structures of pagan society; in fact, the Apostle Paul has frequently been reproached for his social conservatism, as evidenced in his willingness to accept for the time being the institution of slavery and the subordination of women. Yet it was the Christian community's experience of the equal dignity of every member of the congregation which ultimately, by the detour of secular post-Christian humanism to be sure, laid the groundwork for modern conceptions of the rights of man.

The insights of a Christian community may equally prove instructive to the larger society through the example of sober realism about the temptations of power and the persistence of sin in the life even of the righteous. In spite of their convictions about the power that is in the gospel for overcoming sin, the early Christians and their faithful successors in all ages have insisted on the need for mutual fraternal admonition and especially for vigilance to be exercised by the entire congregation with regard to the faithfulness of leaders. Few insights are more fundamental in the political realm than an awareness of the temptations to which even the most righteous and representative of men are subject. Democracy itself is best understood not as the expression of the humanistic "social contract" assuming the goodness of all men, or of most

---

2 In his essay, "Christian Community and Civil Community" (E.T. in W. Herberg, ed., *Community, State, and Church*, Doubleday 1960, p. 149 ff.) Karl Barth has advocated a method of "analogy" for relating church ethics derived from a faith commitment to the lower standards applicable to the civil community. In carrying out the undertaking Barth is not fully consistent; the Church side of the analogy is less important to him and less carefully developed than the civil side; with the *intention* of this approach by analogy we would, however, agree. Cf. our pamphlet, "The Pacifism of Karl Barth," Church Peace Mission, 1964.

18

men, but rather a most realistic way of exercising vigilant supervision over the authority entrusted to a few.

Decisions in the church are, or at least should be, the expression of a convinced consensus arrived at freely as the result of common study within the fellowship of believers.[3] The Holy Spirit is the possession not of a few peculiarly gifted individuals, but of the congregation at large. The unity of the congregation, and not simply a numerical majority of voters, is the true expression of the Spirit's leading in the normal life of the church. Secular analogies to this congregational way of making decisions can be found throughout political and social history, from the town meeting of colonial America to the liberal use of discussion methods in modern American education and in business management.[4] It presupposes the distribution of creative capacities and authority throughout the members of the group in a way that only Christian convictions can ultimately explain.

Not only are there lessons for the outside world from the inner life of the Christian church as a society; a comparable creative impulse should radiate from the church's services to the larger community. The most obvious examples would be the institutions of the school and the hospital, both of which began in Christian history as services rendered by the church, and especially by voluntaristic orders within the church, to the entire society. With the passage of time, the social usefulness of these services became so self-evident that secular authorities took over responsibility for them. The church has continued, in more specialized realms of education and medicine, and also in other areas of social concern, to be the "pilot" creating experimentally new ways of meeting social needs which, once their utility has been proved, can be institutionalized and generalized under the authority of the secular powers. International relief work in favor of the victims of war and natural catastrophe was a voluntary undertaking of Christian groups before it became a governmental concern; voluntary service rendered by young men overseas was carried on under voluntary leadership long before the Peace Corps. If the church senses some proprietary right over these dimensions of service, she will attempt to keep them from

3 The most adequate procedural description of the free church's way of "Reaching Decisions" is the chapter bearing this title in Howard Brinton's *Friends for 300 Years* (Harper, New York, 1952, pp. 99 ff.). The process he describes is by no means limited to Quakerism, though the Friends' tradition has been especially effective in interpreting and maintaining it.

4 Franklin H. Littell, one of the ablest interpreters of what the free-church vision means within the disciplined fellowship, has demonstrated as well its relevance to the larger society. "Christianity does not exist . . . for the service of 'the spirit of democracy' . . . . There is, nevertheless, a nexus between the free church and the free society, and it lies precisely at the method used in decision-making." ("The Work of the Holy Spirit in Group Decisions," *Mennonite Quarterly Review,* Vol. XXXIV No. 2 (April 1960) p. 83.

being taken over by other agencies; if, on the other hand, she understands her ministry as one of constant inventive vision for the good of the larger society, she will rejoice at the evidence that her witness at a given point has been grasped and will move on to new realms where her creativity is more urgently needed.

The Christian church is primarily not a ministerial organization or a conference body, but a host of people called *laymen* in the language of many denominations, whose primary contact with and witness to society is constituted by the fact that they earn their living and raise their families right in the midst of that society. There will be points at which, for reasons of clear conviction, such Christians will be driven to refuse to conform to prevalent patterns of behavior; one relatively clear and extreme example of this kind of nonconformity is conscientious objection to military service. Such a refusal to cooperate, by identifying an issue that is important enough for the concerned person to be willing to run a certain risk and to accept certain sacrifices, is always, at least for the individuals with whom such a person deals and sometimes beyond that circle, a witness about fundamental moral imperatives. It can, however, be no less appropriate to speak of "conscientious participation" in the life of society, by virtue of which the Christian will assist in the solution of problems and the creation of a healthy mentality through the way he does his job and participates in the informal organization of the community. Especially can this be said of those professions which contribute to the organizing of society by defining and working toward moral values at the grass roots level: as a medical or social worker transforming "cases" into persons, as a businessman placing effective community service above immediate profits, as a teacher transmitting to younger generations his sense of what really matters behind the details of his curricular offerings, as a person involved in labor-management relations who seeks some sort of "right" answers instead of maximum selfish gain, as a cog in the bureaucratic and industrial organization willing to take personal responsibility for more than his share of service and who can change the character of a bureaucracy by his personal attitudes, as a good neighbor.

Beyond the implicit witness of placing Christian faithfulness first and of being the church as a model society, the Christian fellowship contributes in numerous indirect ways as well to the development of generally recognized moral standards outside the circle of her own membership. Partly through the Christian education given to young persons who do not themselves become committed church members, and partly through the observable social value of the honesty and industry of Christians, as well as through their refusal to participate in certain social evils, there must be through the years a sort of moral osmosis, whereby the secular world finds itself recognizing certain general moral values to which it has no spiritual or logical commitment.

Yet our assignment is to study the much more direct impact which the church can have upon the way in which the state operates. Independently of the general obligation to evangelize individuals, including statesmen, and in spite of the impropriety of presupposing a Christian commitment on the part of responsible agents of the state, the testimony that the risen Christ is Lord also over the world is to us the reason for speaking to the state, and the biblical witness concerning the reason for the state's continued existence enables us also to guide this testimony with definite standards.

Even when we move beyond the implicit witness which is given by the very example of the church, by her own inner life and her service to the world, and come to speak of particular concerns and criticisms with which she may approach statesmen, the centrality of the church's own experience in this witness should remain clear. This would definitely distinguish the witness of which we here speak from traditional "lobbying" efforts of church and interchurch agencies.

1. The witness to the state must be representative of the church's clear conviction. Legislators and executives have plenty to do with church spokesmen who actually do not speak for their constituencies, and with agencies of government which themselves engineer the artificial public opinion they claim to express. Not only does it seem unlikely that such representations to government can be very effective when they do not truly express a shared conviction; it is even more doubtful whether they are honest.

2. The witness of the church must be consistent with her own behavior. Only if she herself is demonstrably and ethically working on a given problem does the church have a right to speak to others. A racially segregated church has nothing to say to the state about integration. The parallel from prohibition times is clear.[5]

3. The church should speak only when she has something to say.

5 "A church or other free association which has made a discipline binding upon its membership (e.g., plain dress, abstinence, conscientious objection to military service, etc.) has a right to come before fellow citizens with its witness and the recommendation that there be made a general discipline (by law) of what they have experienced and found good. Whether such legislation is then wise, if there is strong objection among other ranks of the citizenry, is another question and must be fought out in the public forum. But in the case of both prohibition and the anti-evolution laws this requirement was not fulfilled: politicians in the churches attempted to secure by public legislation what they were unable to persuade many of their own members was either wise or desirable. In both cases, lacking the authenticity of a genuinely disciplined witness, the Protestant reversion to political action was ultimately discredited, and the churches have not to this day recovered their authority in public life." Franklin H. Littell, *From State Church to Pluralism*, Doubleday, 1962, p. 120.

There should be no sense of a responsibility to "cover the field" with a full gamut of statements on every kind of subject that might be of any moral significance. Only such matters as can be clearly identified by the church as presenting a clear moral challenge or abuse can justify their being given more than perfunctory attention. Speaking within the American denominational framework, it might well be that a predominantly rural church should sense a special responsibility to speak to farm problems—that here it would be worth speaking only if the Christian farmers had something to say that was distinct from the largely self-interested testimonies of agricultural lobbying; that denominations with special experiences in overseas relief might speak of the distribution of surplus commodities in a way others could not; the same might apply to churches experienced in the use of young persons in voluntary services overseas. Only a church doing something about prisoner rehabilitation would have any moral right to speak—or have any good ideas— about prison conditions or parole regulations. It would be quite normal for church agencies working in places of special social aid such as the inner city to have more specific things to say about abuses in the welfare administration, about urban renewal and ward politics, than would the same number of Christians working in a more stable and better governed community.

B. The Relationship Between the Church's Social Witness and Her Testimony to Individuals

A tradition long established in American churches of the evangelical tradition distinguishes quite neatly between "evangelism" on the one hand, understood quite precisely to mean the initial call addressed to individuals to repent and believe and be baptized, and on the other hand the various other kinds of behaving and speaking and worshiping of the church, including her social impact. For some this distinction serves to place the social responsibility of the church in a specific chronological order: first, the evangelization of individuals creates changed persons, who then will become politically effective. Others would use the same distinction in a quite different direction, arguing that man's true need is the initial commitment of faith, so that the church should limit herself to this priority concern and not confuse things by speaking to society at large about all sorts of moral issues. Still others, while affirming the priority of the "evangelistic" ministry, can without inconsistency go on to affirm a secondary or derivative obligation to speak to the political world.[6]

6 Such a distinction was presupposed in the text cited at the beginning of this study (Chap. 1, Note 1). The argument of these pages is a corrective, not to the position sketched there, but to its language.

This distinction is a necessary one. It needs to be said that the church's witness to the social order is not dependent on the number of individuals who are already Christian believers or who come to her for moral guidance. This witness needs to be understood as consistent with the recognition that most rulers are precisely not committed evangelical Christians, and yet that the ethical guidance they are given must somehow make a revelation claim. The distinction is needed to safeguard the biblical understanding of the believers' church, the separation of church and state, and the incompatibility of nonresistance with responsibility for the normal processes of government. We need to distinguish between the ethics of discipleship which are laid upon every Christian believer by virtue of his very confession of faith, and an ethic of justice within the limits of relative prudence and self-preservation, which is all one can ask of the larger society. The distinction is needed to avoid a misunderstanding, perhaps forever banished in its crudest forms with the demise of theological liberalism, but still a latent temptation, namely the tendency to identify the gospel of the kingdom of God with a plan for social betterment independent of the changing men's minds and hearts.

Yet when all this is said there remains something deeply questionable about this distinction, at the very least in its use of language. The restriction of the term *gospel* and of the meaning of *evangelism* to an invitation addressed to individuals is deeply rooted in contemporary American English usage, but is not biblical. It is not the case that a witness to an individual, calling him to conversion with reference to his own personal guilt and the direction of his life, is biblically speaking evangelism whereas the witness either to groups or to persons in social responsibility, calling on them to change their dispositions and do in their offices what God would have them do, is something else. We may look at the meaning of the word *euangellion* in secular Greek, or at the message, "the kingdom of God has come near!" proclaimed in turn by John the Baptist, by Jesus, by His seventy messengers, and by the church at Pentecost; or we could compare the counterparts of this message in Old Testament prophecy. In each case it is clear that the good news announced to the world has to do with the reign of God among men in all their interpersonal relations, and not solely with the forgiveness of sins or the regeneration of individuals. Obviously each individual must make his own decision about whether to respond in obedient faith to this message or to reject it. This, however, must not mean that a concern for individual responses may legitimately hide any of the original social dimensions of the gospel proclamation. What was wrong with the "social gospel" of two generations ago was not that it was social, but that it lacked certain dimensions of the gospel.

All communication is addressed to individuals and calls for individual response. Even communication by means of the mass media, addressed to thousands or even millions of persons, only truly becomes communication if it is heard or read or seen in such a way as to call forth specific responses from individual listeners, readers, or viewers. We must not think of society or the state as some sort of vast and chaotic multitude, but rather as a great number of individuals each responsible for his own response to what he himself hears.

This does not change if instead of addressing a group of people we speak directly to a given statesman of his moral responsibilities. Precisely because the message we express is a derivative of, an element of, a form of the gospel, we must communicate first of all, whatever be the specific political issue with which we are concerned, an awareness of our prior concern for the welfare of this statesman as a man. We are concerned about his own moral integrity, measured first of all by his own moral standards, even though from our perspective his highest ideals might still fall far short of the vision of Christian discipleship. Any such communication to the statesman is thus in a sense pastoral; its presupposition is that one person has the right to be dealt with as a person, as an object of God's and therefore of our esteem, who is honored but also brought into judgment as we speak to him of the implications of divine righteousness.

Thus far Christians of the nonresistant churches have not felt free to speak thus acceptingly to men in responsible positions because of their personal conviction that they themselves could not as faithful Christians serve in these same positions. Not only conservative Mennonite traditions but also highly respected contemporary thinkers argue, as we noted at the outset, that the commitment to discipleship in nonresistance deprives the Christian of anything relevant to say to responsible social leaders. Let us agree for the moment that the starting point of this line of thought, namely that the nonresistant Christian could not be a responsible statesman on high levels, is true without qualification.[7] It still does not logically follow that he is free to judge the statesman from this perspective, for the statesman does not have the same experience, the same information, or the same prior commitment. He might, in fact, have received from other Christian churches, as well as from secular educational sources, a set of convictions that make it impossible for him to understand the relevance of the pacifist vision as anything

---

7 Gordon Kaufman has argued (*The Context of Decision,* Abingdon, 1961, pp. 110ff.; and *Concern* No. 6, 1958, pp. 19 ff.) that even this need not be the case. Unfortunately, Kaufman does not describe the nature of the responsibility a nonresistant Christian can seek, its limits, or the reasons for it, with sufficient precision to permit serious evaluation.

but a sign of total spiritual emigration from the surrounding society. This fact, that the responsible statesman does not share the non-resistant believer's information or commitment, is the reason he needs to be spoken to. It might very well be, if this man is engaged in an activity that has generally not been thought reprehensible, but which a more sensitive or more informed Christian conscience would not permit, that in the process of responding to the gospel he might come to the conclusion that his office is incompatible with his faith. But it is improper to begin with this conclusion. It is impossible to impose this logic on him before beginning the conversation.

On whatever level we find a man in the effort to speak to him, what we ask of him is that he accept the gospel. It would be easy to carry the earlier formal distinction between evangelism of individuals and critique of society on into a substantial distinction between the gospel and its call to personal conversion on one hand and on the other some other kind of decent moral standards applied to those who have rejected the gospel. Then we would wrongly understand the witness to a person in authority as a sort of second best, as if we had first called him to believe in Jesus Christ, and then, when he had said he would not, we would go on to plead, "Well, all right then, but will you please at least be decent and honest?" What we ask of him does not cease to be gospel by virtue of the fact that we relate it to his present available options. It is rather the gospel itself in relationship to his present situation, that situation in turn being determined largely by his earlier disobedience. If, for example, a subordinate officer in the Korean War had been challenged to treat his prisoners of war according to the Geneva Convention, or if a French intelligence officer in Algeria had been challenged not to torture innocent suspects, the only way he could have responded to this challenge—even though it was placed before him fully in terms of his present military involvement and of military justice—would be to take a step of obedience which would be costly, would be an act of repentance, would be a leap of faith, would bring upon him suffering and reproach, would be possible only in the strength of the Holy Spirit and in the name of Jesus Christ. This call to him therefore differs from that which the conscientious objector is following only in the level of involvement in which the message finds the man to whom it speaks, and in the length of time which each in his place has had to think through in detail the implications of Christian obedience. Whether this one step in the right direction would lead the army officer in Korea ultimately to an experience of complete commitment, regeneration, and church membership is no more an open question than for an individual who records a decision in a rescue mission to take the first steps; yet in the latter case no one rejects the professed faith because it is not yet fully articulate.

25

C. Democracy

Since the purpose of the present study is to demonstrate the possibility of speaking to the state from the posture of New Testament nonresistance, rather than arguing the case for nonresistance in its own right, this is not the place to examine in detail the extremely current modern argument that the development of democracy has so changed the context of social responsibility that the biblical position is not only wrong but, in fact, irrelevant and inconceivable in a society where every citizen must affirm, as in another age only Louis XIV could do, "I myself am the state!"

It will have to suffice here to indicate that, however broadly it may be believed, the thesis of the fundamental novelty of democratic government is neither historically nor theologically convincing. It is still the fact that some men exercise power over others, with a view partly to personal benefit and partly to less selfish purposes. In many kinds of society democracy is preferable to any other form of government; this does not change the fact that even in such societies some men wield the sword and others do not.

If we refuse the mythological explanation of democracy as a fundamentally new kind of social order, we can rejoice in the immensely increased possibilities which it provides of speaking to those who exercise power; the decentralization of authority, the election of legislators by a local constituency, and the constitutional and judicial controls on abuse of authority are all factors which oblige the men in power to listen to criticism with a greater degree of seriousness than in the age of absolutist monarchs.[8]

The elective process, and in a general sense even the legislative process (especially on the national level, where the overwhelming power of bureaucracy is the most predominant) may thus best be

---

[8] The simple assumption of a New Testament ecclesiological orientation in the present paper has been motivated by the narrowly defined goals of the study and not by a lack of awareness of the challenges which this position needs to face. Some of these challenges are logically circular, such as the argument that the New Testament strategy is no longer possible or effective or socially responsible. Such concepts as "possible," "effective," "responsible," are themselves value judgments on issues to which the New Testament itself speaks. To argue with them would, therefore, involve excursions into philosophical theology to clarify the nature of biblical authority and the relevance of the incarnation.

Some historically based arguments are less circular. The most serious of these is probably the claim that Christianity's acceptance as the official religion of the Roman Empire must lead to a different social strategy. To this issue we have attempted to speak in "The Otherness of the Church," *Mennonite Quarterly Review*, Vol. XXXV, Oct. 1961, p. 286 ff. Still others would argue from the changes that have come over the state as it has become involved ever more deeply in economics, in education, in welfare services. These stages are profound but, we would argue, do not modify the significance of the sword-bearing activities of the state. Only the changes in the meaning of the politics resulting from the development of democracy belong within our present treatment. Even here, it may be challenged whether the changes are as great as they are made to seem. The medieval serf, though technically the slave of the lord in the castle, could by well-timed local uprisings win significant concessions; whereas today the voter is often given no real choices.

understood not as final and responsible participation in the making of government decisions about how the sword of the state is to be used, and still less as morally blameworthy involvement in executing those decisions; but rather as one relatively effective way the subject population has of making its likes and dislikes known.

For the idea that the voter himself is making the decision to have any real validity, it would be necessary for the options presented to the electorate to include all the possible choices. In a two-party system this is never the case. The voter chooses not a position of principle but the less objectionable of two competing oligarchies.

Understanding the franchise as a means of communicating to the bearers of political authority underlines how seriously the Christian witness is compromised by the fact that for most Christians the decision about how to vote is not the expression of any careful evaluation of what needs to be said to the authorities; the decision to abstain from voting is likewise seldom evaluated with a view to its communicating something.

This is not to argue that participation in the elective process cannot be a real involvement in the power struggle; certainly for many of those who are politically active it is intentionally that. This is clearly the case, for instance, in those countries where the Roman Catholic Church favors one particular party. The purpose in such cases is not to speak to those in authority but to become politically powerful and to use that power in the interest of one's own goals. When this is the intent of political action, the action must be judged by that intent and not only by its real effect. We would therefore have to say clearly that those who in this way seek to gain power in order to implement their religious vision have chosen (probably consciously) a strategy hardly reconcilable with that of the New Testament church. But this does not change our present argument; namely, that those who think participation in the legislative and elective processes to be major involvement in the wielding of the sword are probably mistaken and that it would be quite possible from the position of New Testament nonresistance to use selectively these means of communication without any compromise being implied.[9] Not only the voter but, in fact, even the

9 It has been argued by some in local tribunals evaluating the conscientious objector status of young draftees that voting is a privilege, the enjoyment of which commits the recipient to an obligation to defend the state in whose government he participates. We have shown that such an understanding of the vote is not politically realistic. If, however, it is held with great conviction by one's neighbor, then our understanding of the vote as a witness would also include respect for the neighbor's views and would therefore make it possible that nonresistant Christians would abstain from the use of the franchise, not because it is intrinsically wrong or inconsistent with their nonresistance, but because of the offense it would give to those who would see in it a moral inconsistency. In still other countries, especially the "people's democracies" and some of the Latin American Republics, the vote is a legal obligation. In such places the normal effect of the "submission" of Romans 13 would probably be to vote; abstention at the cost of possible punishment might be one of the more normal channels of protest against government injustice.

legislator, if he has no concern for his re-election or for developing a power bloc, could without compromise conceive of his office more as an occasion to speak to the authorities than as being an agent of the government. Whether such a nonresistant candidate would ever be elected and whether the investment of his efforts in such a context would be good stewardship of his vision and energy are questions on a quite different level, which might well lead to a decision against seeking or occupying legislative office. Perhaps a more fruitful investment of the same amount of concern and expertise would be achieved in the role of a journalist or lobbyist. That such a function would be conceivable without compromise is, however, a significant corrective to the current understanding that the Christian who eschews the sword is thereby implicitly condemned, if he would be consistent, to complete withdrawal from the political process.

This understanding of the franchise as a channel of testimony must, if taken seriously, lead to much more serious study of the issues really at stake and of the meaning of both voting and abstention. There would ideally need to be common deliberation and common action if the Christian witness is not to be a testimony more to confusion than to truth. Abstention as a testimony against corrupt politicians who give the electors no tolerable options because no real issues are at stake, or because the Christian brotherhood does not see clearly what needs to be said, would in many cases be more responsible than casting a vote without conviction or information or for sentimental or selfish reasons.

4. GENERAL CONSIDERATIONS OF ETHICAL THEORY

A. Church and World, the Locus of the Duality

BEFORE TURNING TO A discussion of the types of counsel or criticism which Christians may address to the state, we must discuss the attitude and the method involved in such an approach.

The most significant axiom of this approach to the state will be its clear recognition that Christian ethics is for Christians. This statement is by no means a useless tautology. The major ethical traditions of the Western world, as indicated above in another connection, have by and large held in common the conviction that, since Christian moral standards reflect the will of God, they must apply equally to all men and to society as a whole. When we ask the question, Are Christian principles relevant in the social order? it would seem impossible to say "no" since this would mean shutting God out of His world. If, on the other hand, we answer simply "yes," the conclusion has seemed inescapable that therefore Christian moral standards must be imposed, whether by force or by persuasion, on all of society.

It is at this point that the New Testament view of the relationship of church and world was renewed by the early Anabaptists and Quakers. The question, Are Christian principles relevant to the social order? is misleading in its simplicity, since it presupposes that the permanent and objective element in ethical truth is a set of disincarnate principles, so that these principles may be transposed from one frame of reference to another without further thought. This is the fallacy of moralism. It is necessary in our age of existentialism and contextualism to insist that the good does not depend on a whim or a passing intuition; in this context the argument for principles still has value. But a great deal does depend on the identity of the moral agent. Christian ethics is for the Christian, who— if he will—disposes of the resources of love, repentance, the willingness to sacrifice, and the enabling power of the Holy Spirit, within the supporting fellowship of the church. Whether or not, or in what sense, non-Christians or the non-Christian society *should* love, forgive, and otherwise behave like Christians is a speculative question. The spiritual resources for making such redeemed behavior a real possibility are lacking.

Thus the fundamental duality with which the Christian speaking to the environing society must reckon is not the difference between church and state as social institutions, nor between interpersonal relations on the face-to-face level and large group relations or between legalism and "playing by ear,"—although these differences will ultimately also be involved—but the difference between faith and unbelief as the presuppositions of his ethical message. To his Christian brethren the Christian addresses a testimony whose sole norm is Jesus Christ and whose adequate basis is the faith commitment of the brother spoken to. Outside the circle of faith, the presupposition cannot be the commitment of the individual spoken to and challenged, but only Christ's objective claim on him.

As we shall see later in another connection, Christian ethical thought has attempted to deal with social problems in one of two general ways. On the one hand there have been the dualistic approaches, of which the Roman Catholic distinction between "mandates" and counsels," or the Lutheran "two kingdoms" (better "two regimes") may be taken as classical historical expressions. Here it is clearly recognized that for the operation of society there must be moral standards falling short of the righteousness of

Christ, but ways are found for explaining the adequacy of these lower standards as guides for *Christian* behavior, at least for certain Christians or certain portions of the Christian's life.[1]

As a protest against this dualistic view, which seemed to make room too readily for sin, the Puritan tradition has tended to insist on a single ethical standard applied to all men and all situations. Immanuel Kant is typical of the Puritan tradition in ethics, when he establishes the possibility of applying the same moral norms to all men as the touchstone for identifying the "categorical imperative." Unless one can say that a given value should be sought by all men, it is not, he argues, a valid goal even for oneself. Kant's purpose is clear and understandable. He wants to be able to claim that a valid moral imperative is universal and objective; he therefore seeks for an imperative which will not be dependent on the individual. Yet the Christian is dependent, according to the testimony of the New Testament, both for knowing the good and for being able to do it, on personal repentance, forgiveness, and regeneration. Realism forbids that we assume any such personal orientation when we speak to society at large.

It is within the same Puritan tradition that traditional liberal pacifism has argued that, since war is wrong, it should not take place. Proceeding directly from the incompatibility of war with the Sermon on the Mount, pacifism has found itself unable to formulate demands and standards which statesmen could recognize as realistic possibilities. This is not because the pacifists misunderstood the Sermon on the Mount; it is because the statesmen were operating in a realm where the presupposition of the Sermon on the Mount, namely, the faith of the committed individual making an ethical decision as part of the people of God, did not obtain.

This Puritan tradition, attempting to apply one set of moral standards to all kinds of persons, seems to be the near opposite of the dualistic approach. Yet, in a deeper sense, these two positions agree. Both are concerned about finding a moral standard for society. They assume that they know what society is and that there exists a set of standards which will directly apply to the ethical problems which a society or a state must face. The pacifist says the only standards are those of the Sermon on the Mount; therefore the state should obey the Sermon on the Mount. The Calvinist says the standards which apply are those of the Old Testament theocracy and proceeds to apply them. The dualist says that because of sin there must be another set of standards than those that apply to individual Christians and that these standards can be found in some source other than the gospel

---

[1] For a more complete comparative study of typical approaches to this problem with the help of graphic representation, cf. below Chapter 7, p. 57 ff.

(whether this be in the Old Testament, in reason, or somewhere else). All agree that they are seeking to develop an "ethic for the state" that can stand alone.

The position which we would here argue seeks to be more faithful to the example of the New Testament. It fits none of these patterns, since in searching for a way to speak of an "ethic for the state" we do not believe that such an ethic can stand alone. With the New Testament we shall affirm the necessity of orders and organization based on power in social relations. This is the result not first of God's having willed that it be so, but only of human sin. The Anabaptists described this "duality without dualism" by speaking of the sword as part of the world "outside the perfection of Christ"; the phrase "inside the perfection of Christ" designated both the Christian church as a body and Christian ethics as a new ethical level. Both the violent action of the state (Romans 13:4) and the nonresistance of the Christian (12:9) are ways of God's acting in the world. These two aspects of God's work are not distinguished by God's having created two realms but by the actual rebelliousness of men. A similar position was taken by the early Friends, even though contemporary Quakerism is renowned for its political pacifism. In Robert Barclay's *Apology* we read:

As to what relates to the present Magistrates of the Christian World, albeit we deny them not altogether the name of Christians, because of the publick Profession they make of Christ's Name, yet we may boldly affirm, that they are far from the Perfection of the Christian Religion: because in the State in which they are . . . they have not come to the pure Dispensation of the Gospel. And, therefore, while they are in that condition, we shall not say, That War, undertaken upon a just occasion, is altogether unlawful to them. For even as Circumcision, and the other Ceremonies, were for a season permitted to the Jews, not because they were either necessary of themselves, or lawful at that time, after the Resurrection of Christ; but because that Spirit was not yet raised up in them, whereby they could be delivered from such Rudiments; so the present Confessors of the Christian Name, who are yet in the mixture, and not in the patient Suffering Spirit, are not yet fitted for this form of Christianity, and therefore cannot be undefending themselves, until they attain that Perfection. But for such, whom Christ has brought hither, it is not lawful to defend themselves by Arms, but they ought over all to trust to the Lord."[2]

In spite of differences in form from the Anabaptist phrasing we have here the same synthesis between a) the insistence that only the defenseless way is the right one and b) the idea that for those who are not ready to go all this way there is another category of ethical

2 *An Apology for the True Christian Divinity as the Same Is Held Forth, and Preached, by the People, Called in Scorn, Quakers. . . .* London, 1676. Most accessible in Eleanor Price Mather (ed.), *Barclay in Brief*, Pendle Hill Pamphlet No. 28, second printing 1948, p. 63.

imperatives within which there may also be judgments of "just" and "unjust."

The difference between Christian ethics for Christians and a Christian ethic for the state is therefore due to duality not of realms or levels, but of responses. Where God speaks to the reconciled and committed believer, the command to "be minded as it befits someone who is in Christ" (Phil. 2) takes into consideration all the possibilities of the Holy Spirit and the church. When God's will is communicated to man or men in their rebellion, neither God nor His ultimate will changes, but His current demands take into account the nonbelief of the addressee (just as any truly *personal* communication encounters the addressee where he is) and therefore stay within other limits of possibility.

B. Ideals, Principles, and Situation Ethics

Since we cannot say that God has any "proper" pattern in mind to which unbelief should conform, the Christian witness to the state will not be guided by an imagined pattern of ideal society such as is involved in traditional conceptions of the "just state," the "just war," or "the due process of law." An ideal or even a "proper" society in a fallen world is by definition impossible. The Christian speaks not of how to describe, and then to seek to create the ideal society, but of how the state can best fulfill its responsibilities in a fallen society.

The Christian witness will therefore always express itself in terms of specific criticisms, addressed to given injustices in a particular time and place, and specific suggestions for improvements to remedy the identified abuse. This does not mean that if the criticisms were heard and the suggestions put into practice, the Christian would be satisfied; rather, a new and more demanding set of criticisms and suggestions would then follow. There is no level of attainment to which a state could rise, beyond which the Christian critique would have nothing more to ask; such an ideal level would be none other than the kingdom of God.

Traditional social ethics attempted to apply principles which it was held were somehow built into the nature of man or of the social order. The approach sketched above will need to operate without such principles, not because definite and knowable understandings of God's will do not exist, but because such insights are known only in Christ and their application is therefore possible only mediately. Consequently, our speaking to the state will call for the use of middle axioms. These concepts will translate into meaningful and concrete terms the general relevance of the lordship of Christ for a given social ethical issue. They mediate between the general principles of Christological ethics and the con-

32

crete problems of political application. They claim no metaphysical status, but serve usefully as rules of thumb to make meaningful the impact of Christian social thought.[3]

Social-ethical thought has in the past tended to sway between a relativism that challenges the existence of any standards beyond the good intention of the person making a decision and a natural law concept which supposes that we can know clearly a pattern of ideal order which it is our assignment to impose on our society. The conception of middle axioms avoids these alternatives. It permits meaningful communication of a significant Christian social critique without involving extended speculation about the metaphysical value of the principles appealed to.

C. General Revelation

Interminable debate has raged about the concepts "order of nature" and "natural law." These terms have for a long time been the vehicle on which value judgments could be introduced into ethical discussion without needing support in revelation. The claim, at least for those who cared at all about revelation, was that the order of nature is itself a vehicle of revelation, parallel or complementary or preliminary to revelation in Christ and Scripture. Yet historical study shows that it has been possible to understand under *order of nature* just about anything a philosopher wanted; stoicism or epicureanism, creative evolution or political restorationism, Puritan democrary or Aryan dictatorship. We shall do well to avoid thinking of the order of nature as a source of any kind of revelation.[4] Yet at the same time we must recognize that there exists also in the unredeemed world an order, a relation to Him who ordains, and who is none other than our Redeemer. This is the concept of order (*taxis*) and duty (*opheilein*) which runs through Romans 13:1-7 and which we have referred to as the reign of Christ. On the basis of revelation we can thus speak of a structure of society whose main lines we may ascertain—from revelation, not from nature—and which will be the framework of our judgments about ethics for states. This structure is, however, not a stable ideal order, but an *ordering*, a historical mediation

---

3 The term *middle axiom* was made current especially by the preparatory materials for the social ethics discussion at the World Council of Churches' Amsterdam General Assembly in 1948. The term has two meanings; these middle axioms are halfway between meaninglessly broad generalities and unrealistically precise prescriptions; their claim to authority is also midway between absolute moral principles and mere pragmatic common sense: ". . . a middle ground between a Christian view which offered no general directions to the Christian for his decisions with regard to social and political institutions, and the view which tried to identify the mind of Christ too simply with specific . . . programmes" (Reinhold Niebuhr, p. 28 in *The Church and the Disorder of Society*). We can add a third shade of meaning; they mediate between the norms of faith and the situation conditioned by unbelief. Such middle axioms are the subject of our Chapter 5.

4 Cf. below p. 76 ff.

between continued rebellion and the orderliness of the kingdom to come.

In rejecting the idea that the norms for the social order are revealed in some order of creation, we do not mean to deny the foundation of human society within the creative intention of God. What we do deny is that the order of creation can explain to us a) why and how the *sword,* i.e., the calculated measuring out of evil, can be necessary, and b) just what standards distinguish between proper and improper exercise of justice.

The ambiguity of the theory of natural law lies in its confusion of the *is* with the *ought.* If the nature from which we read the obligations of men or of the state or of the head of the family or the worker is empirical, i.e., if nature is "things as they are," then we can very definitely establish at any place and time just what are the structures of nature; but they can then not serve as a critique or a moral imperative. If, on the other hand, the "nature of things" is some sort of philosophical essence to be distinguished from things as they are, it can have the character of the moral imperative, but it cannot be ascertained empirically in nature.[5] Most philosophical users of natural law do choose the latter alternative; they see in it a genuine moral imperative for man or an institution to become what it or he is not yet; but then it is clear that the truth claim of such a philosophical approach needs to be confronted with the revelation claims of the biblical witness, and the essentialist approach is in itself foreign to the historical thrust of the biblical witness.[6]

If the truth of revelation is not arbitrary, but grounded in the reality of Christ's dominion, then the application of these middle axioms should correspond with the most accurate and impartial descriptions of historical reality. The more objective a historian or social critic becomes, the more competent and broadly informed his analysis, the closer his conclusions should correspond to our middle axioms. Thus the study of history provides a way of checking the axioms and, conversely, Christian insight can provide unique assistance toward the objective understanding of history. The works of the Christian historian Herbert Butterfield are remarkable examples of this creative interplay of Christian insight and historical objectivity. Butterfield demonstrates that only a Christian orientation permits a truly fair understanding of the facts of history. This is first of all the case because honest objectivity, respect for the truth apart from oneself, is possible only with the fundamental

---

5 The traditional temptation of Lutheranism has been to make an *is* into an *ought* by interpreting Romans 13 as a value judgment on particular states. "There are no powers which are not under God" they took to mean "Whatever government you have is good." Cf. below pp. 60, 71.

6 Cf. below p. 81, note 8.

abandon of self-defense involved in Christian faith; secondly, the specifically Christian virtue of forgiveness should make it possible to see that even the apparent villain in historical conflicts is subject to causes not wholly his fault, and capable of some good; thirdly, the virtue of repentance permits accepting for oneself or one's class or nation a part of the blame for what goes wrong in history; further, the Christian hope makes it possible to approach the study of history in the deep faith that it will somehow make sense, that there will be signs of long-term purposiveness and of justice; and the Christian concern for human dignity, in the concrete form of the neighbor rather than in institutions or ideologies, enables the Christian historian to seek the meaning of history in personal and moral values, freed from the temptation to interpret primarily the story of regimes and sovereignties. This enumeration of ways in which Christian insight qualifies the historian—or rather *may* and *should* qualify him—could be extended; but this much should suffice not only to indicate that the Christian's moral commitment should make him a better historian and social analyst, but also to permit the corollary thesis that the properly objective analysis of events will test the rightness of the Christian's moral evaluation.[7]

5. THE CRITERIA
OF POLITICAL JUDGMENT

THE MAIN BURDEN of the present paper has been the logically preliminary portion. The fundamental problem is not how to express the Christian's analysis of political events, since the judgment of Christians who are well informed will often differ little in substance from the intelligent judgment of other social critics, but rather how to understand within a Christian framework by what right such a judgment may be formulated by Christians and addressed to social leaders. Our claim has been that the Christian understanding of history, and especially of the relationship of church and world, gives the key to such a ministry. We now proceed to a selective listing of middle axioms, with the intention not so much of arguing for all or any one of them, as of using such samples to elucidate the general stance already discussed.

7 A masterful exposition of the light which Christian insight may well cast on political analysis is provided by Herbert Butterfield, *Christianity and History* (London, Bell, 1954). Most of what Butterfield says, once he has said it, would be quite acceptable to a competent non-Christian historian; yet it is said and said first and best by Butterfield because he is a Christian.

A. The state, or more generally the organization of society, exists according to the message of the New Testament for the sake of the work of the church and not vice versa. Much recent discussion of "Christian responsibility" has been extremely confusing—rather than definitely false—because of its failure to clarify the standards by which such responsibility should be measured. If these standards should be understood to signify Christians' accepting the ultimate priority of the work of the state over that of the church, then such responsibility would be treason to their own higher commission.[1] The validity of our witness to society, including the critical address to the state and the statesman, hangs on the firmness with which the church keeps her central message at the center: her call to every man to turn to God and her call to those who have turned to God to live in love. If she fails to keep this call to personal commitment at the center of her life and work, her prophetic witness to society is either utopianism or demagoguery.

We may note in passing that the term *prophetic witness* frequently employed in this connection is, in fact, improper. We here use it only as a concession to established usage and shall generally prefer some such term as *social critique*. In both Old and New Testaments, the prophet speaks not to the world but to the people of God. A rigorously proper theology, therefore, would speak of the prophetic work of the church as going on within her midst and would understand the critical witness to the world rather as the exercise of the kingly office of Christ and His church.

B. Our first fundamental criterion for historical analysis will be the concept of order which we have already seen to be presupposed in Romans 13. First Timothy 2 uses the term *peace;* Romans 13 and 1 Peter 2 indicate that this state obtains when the innocent are protected and the guilty punished; these are the standards for the legitimacy of the function of magistrate. We may thus conclude that the state never has a blanket authorization to use violence. The use of force must be limited to the police function, i.e., guided

---

1 The strong emotional appeal of the word *responsibility* and the extreme pejorative ring of the epithet *irresponsible* have avoided the need for precise definition of the virtue in question. Rigorous analysis of the function the term discharges in the ethical argument of the Niebuhrian school would probably confirm that there is no more exact meaning than that *responsibility signifies a commitment to consider the survival, the interests, or the power of one's own nation, state, or class as taking priority over the survival, interests, or power of other persons or groups, of all of humanity, of the "enemy," or of the church.* If it does *not* mean this, the concept of responsibility cannot prove what it is being used to prove in current debate. If it *does* mean this, it is clearly questionable at two points: a) the priority of state over church; b) the priority of oneself and one's own group over others or the "enemy," as locus both of value and of decision. This basic egotism of the responsibility argument is clothed as a form of altruism. Far from being selfish, it is a sacrificial attitude; it renounces self-defense and defends others instead: the helpless, the innocent, the social order itself. And yet it is uniformly one's own social order, never the opposing one; one's own family, not that of the brother across the border, which is served so heroically.

by fair judicial processes, subject to recognized legislative regulation, and safeguarded in practice against its running away with the situation. Only the absolute minimum of violence is therefore in any way excusable. The state has no general authorization to use the sword independently of its commission to hold violence to a minimum.

C. The danger is seldom that the state authorities will fail to do their job of policing. The universal temptation is rather to overdo this function. Instead of seeing itself as the guardian of the stability of a "tolerable balance of egoisms" within which the work of the church and the socially constructive efforts of men of good will can go forward, the policeman or the statesman comes to consider himself as being responsible for bringing into existence an ideal order. Since the consequences of fundamental structural changes can never be fully foreseen, such efforts to organize the ideal society from the top will always be less successful than hoped; but what matters more is that the pretention to be, or to be in the process of becoming the ideal society, is pride, the one sin that most surely leads to a fall, even already within history. Thus the state need not ask to be worshiped to be on its way to becoming demonic; it is sufficient that it place the authority of its police arm behind its pretention to represent an ideal order, and it is already making religious claims.[2]

"Religious" self-glorification of the state has often been thought of as the most terrible, and for some the only, wrong a state can commit.[3] It has been all the more easy to agree on the extreme definition because such an extreme case is practically impossible to measure objectively. Most German Christians did not observe this extreme in Adolf Hitler; Karl Barth was sure it was there. Karl Barth today does not observe it in Communism; others think he should.

But it is not only the vagueness and arbitrariness of the criterion

2 We used in passing the term *demonic* as it has come to be used by the Niebuhrians to designate a special degree of rebelliousness. The idea is that creaturely values may be kept in their modest place; then they are not demonic. Or they may absolutize themselves, becoming claimants to the loyalty due to God alone (cf. especially Reinhold Niebuhr, *Human Destiny*, Scribners 1948, pp. 110 ff.). Then they are demonic and must be resisted. This usage is unbiblical. *Daimon* and the other comparable, more frequent biblical terms, refer to a category of beings, not to a value judgment. To say that a state is demonic then means not that that state is rebellious (in contrast to other states thought to be non-rebellious) but only that it has a kind of independent being of its own. A hypothetical just, sober, and modest state would still be in the order of the demonic. (Cf. below a parallel confusion as to the state's entering or escaping from the lordship of Christ, Chap. 8 Note 3).

3 Cf. O. Cullman, *The State in the New Testament*, p. 78: "In the Roman state emperor worship is the point at which the state exceeds its proper bounds, at which it poses as a redemptive institution. . . ." Cf. Karl Barth (in W. Herberg, ed., op. cit. Chap. 3, Note 2): "When the state begins to claim 'love,' it is in process of becoming a church, the church of a false god, and thus an unjust state." Cf. *ibid.* pp. 115-118.

of self-deification that makes it suspect. There is no clear reason that an offense against the first commandment of the law should be in a different category from the rest. Idolatry need not be confessed, apostasy need not be cultic, to be expressive of essential rebellion against God. The real error of this religious criterion for the apostasy of any state is not the most extreme evil it would identify, but the implication that there can be an exercise of violent dominion which is *not* intrinsically self-glorifying, that there can be a nationalism which is *not* idolatry or a total war which is *not* intrinsic evidence of the state's absolutizing itself; i.e., that the sword is itself not a part of the Fall.

D. The Christian social critique will always speak in terms of available, or at least conceivable, alternatives. It will not request from the state the establishment of a perfect society, but will call rather for the elimination of specific visible abuses. When the doctrine of the so-called lesser evil is used to advocate moral compromise for the Christian, it is illegitimate for a number of reasons. Even in the political realm it can lead to serious misunderstanding, if one's judgment as to which evil is lesser did not involve an exhaustive examination of available alternatives (what is to be sought is not the *lesser* but the *least* evil). It is further inacceptable if it weighs evils against each other on the basis of non-Christian or selfish conceptions of relative evil.[4]

Beyond these misconceptions, however, there is a very real sense in which the lesser-evil mentality is correct. What we ask *of the state* is not the total elimination of all evils, but a possible elimination of evils which are presently identifiable and particularly offensive. The prophetic witness of Christian social critique, in the great days of Puritanism, Quakerism, Wesleyanism, and revivalism —and even in its Old Testament foreshadowings—always has worked most effectively by combating one visible sin at a time, and has led to the greatest confusion and ineffectiveness when conceived as proposing the establishment of an ideal order. When, through a confusion with nonbiblical lines of thought, an ideal

---

4 Cf. *The Christian and War*, Historic Peace Churches, Amsterdam, 1958, p. 12ff. As examples of such comparison of evils, illegitimate not because it compares evils but because it compares them according to criteria independent of Christian insight, we may cite:

a) the popular slogan, "better dead than Red," pretending to measure the survival of the human race against the survival of a given political order, as if any political order were valuable apart from humanity's survival. The emotional tug of this slogan comes from the common judgment that it is heroic to die for the fatherland. At the very best this idea is pagan and not Christian; but most often it is hypocritical cover for the intention not to die but to kill for the fatherland.

b) the related slogan, "Slavery is worse than death"; measuring illogically an evil one would *inflict* in war against an evil one would *suffer* on losing the war.

"Better dead than Red" at least faces real possibilities and poses in a dramatic way a possible real choice. Yet even here "better share the guilt of mass murder than lose political sovereignty" would be the sober way to put it. It also assumes that warfare itself or prolonged military buildups will effectively avoid collectivism.

order is demanded, the "prophet" afterward discovers that he has played into the hands of secularizing and demonizing influences. When, on the other hand, he exposes one injustice at a time, pointing each time to a less evil way which the statesman can understand and follow, there can be a real improvement in the tolerability of the social compromise and thus in a certain sense progress. A comparison between the political morality of the Anglo-Saxon and some Latin-American countries makes it clear that such progress is possible. We should not confuse this progress with the attainment of the good life, nor assume that the personal or social salvation of man is thereby achieved. The ideal order would require sinless men; by definition it cannot be attained in this age. At the same time that some dimensions show progress (e.g., Anglo-Saxon civil liberties) others become steadily worse (militarism).[5]

The fact that the Christian social critique is therefore always relative means that it is always misunderstood when either its friends or its adversaries attempt to carry it to its logical conclusion. Since the Christian social critique finds its standards in the kingdom of God—for there are no other standards—the logical conclusion of their consistent application would be the Kingdom; but the whole reason for our present discussion is the fact that the Kingdom is not an available possibility, lying beyond both the capacities and intentions of fallen society. To ask, therefore, Where could this lead? is to distort the nature of the problem. The fact that the world to which we speak is in rebellion guarantees that the Christian social critique can never lead too far. The world can be challenged, at the most, on one point at a time, to take one step in the right direction, to approximate in a slightly greater degree the righteousness of love.

We may observe the symbolic demonstration of this point in the fact that anarchy is only a word, a grammatical invention, an imaginary concept. There is no such thing as anarchy. There are varying forms of government, from tyranny to the constitutional democracy; there are varying degrees of centralization of power, from the world empire through the nation to the independent tribe. There may even be government through the interaction of rival powers as in a guerrilla war or where criminal underworld is highly organized. There may be variation in the effectiveness of control, from total regimentation to a weak power barely able to pursue the least criminals. Authority may be delegated or seized,

---

5 The eschatological significance of the church's witness is not limited to the prediction of ultimate judgment and victory. If truly the earnest of the promised triumph has been given to our age, then the discerning both of real "progress" and of real cumulation of evil is not only permissible but mandatory. The dynamic of Bible faith has (with time and sometimes indirectly) created for the first time a sense of world community; it has freed whole peoples from primitive-pagan superstitions in favor of a more rational world view and let the "post-religious" world come of age; it has built schools and factories, fed, and healed. But progress is also regression. The house swept clean is soon inhabited again. Technology becomes prideful and self-confident; the Marxists (or the bankers) become tyrants. The "Peace of God" becomes The Crusade.

it may be exercised wisely or stupidly, efficiently or clumsily, overtly or undercover. But there is always authority, and where it seems to function too little for the welfare and stability of society, the reason is never that the critique coming from the direction of Christian love has been too effective.[6]

E. When we affirm that the real meaning of history is on a level different from that of the function of the state, we do not mean only that the function of the church within society is to preach the gospel. It is also the case that there exists a level of human values, not specifically Christian but somehow subject to Christian formative influences, where the real movement of history takes place. These values cannot be and should not be made subject to the control of the state nor should it be thought that they are valuable only insofar as they contribute to the state. We refer here not only to "cultural" activities, but to the entire fabric of human togetherness — to attitudes of honesty and mutual respect, hard work and clean thinking, unselfishness and tolerance, which the Christian witness creates not only among committed church members, but also by what we have called "moral osmosis" among its sympathizers and among the children of Christians even if these children do not themselves choose the path of discipleship. Herbert Butterfield refers to this entire realm with the term *imponderables,* meaning that the values in question are not directly subject to scientific prediction and governmental manipulation.[7] Positive achievements in this field can come only when the life of society goes forward with a minimum both of disruption and of moral management from above; i.e., within the relative peace and freedom which it is the function of government to preserve. The Christian social critique will therefore distrust every proposal to sacrifice personal values in the present for future institutional benefits, especially if the making of the sacrifice and the later achievement of the good purpose are entrusted to the political authorities and envisaged as the establishment of a better order. A better order will come if, when, and insofar as it can come on earth, when the political apparatus is held in check and where the church is thereby most free to carry out her first task of evangelization and discipleship and her second task of witness to the social order.

F. The Christian speaking to social issues should expect most often to be taking the unpopular side. It is not easy to distinguish the valid reasons for such partisanship from the sympathy for the "other side" which is a usual expression of the nonconformist mentality and from the distrust of present leadership which is almost

---

6 J. Yoder, *The Christian and the Death Penalty,* Newton, 1961, p. 12.

7 Butterfield uses the phrase especially in *Christianity, Diplomacy, and War* (Abingdon-Cokesbury, no date) pp. 79 ff., 109; but the conviction that the happenings that really matter are not on the political surface penetrates all Butterfield's writings.

instinctive in certain social classes. Yet the fact that there are some improper reasons for being always on the side of the underdog should not drive us to identify with the majority or with those in power. The witness to the state of which we are speaking is, by virtue of the nonresistant Christian commitment which it presupposes, by necessity the expression of a small minority. Such a group cannot speak to every conceivable issue and adds nothing significant when what it has to say is no different from what others say. We have further observed that the Christian witness does not provide any foundations for government, either practically or philosophically, but that the Christian rather accepts the powers that be and speaks to them in a corrective way. It is when we speak to those in power and to the dominant majority groups in the population that we plead the case of the minorities and the absent; this does not mean that if we were speaking to the minority groups themselves we should be uncritical or flattering.

The universal biblical concern for "the widow and the orphan" expresses the awareness that in any society certain categories of persons will be excluded from the economic and social privileges of the strong. The much-heralded welfare state is not likely to change this fact. The dependency that can be fostered by the dole system, the establishment of routine norms to avoid fraud, which thereby also eliminate some cases of genuine need, the concentration on objectivity, the placing of persons in categories of neediness, and the local political abuse of welfare resources will always leave the serious needs of some persons unmet. A concern, for example, for those needy persons, the support or rehabilitation of whom does not justify itself by making them economically productive, is not only an immediate duty of the Christian fellowship; pointing to their need is at the same time a witness reminding those in power of the continuing injustices of their regime.

But the biblical concern was not limited to the widow and orphan as representing those persons who find themselves at a disadvantage within a given cultural group; the same responsibility extended to the "stranger." Here the specifically Christian ethical commitment is even more significant, for the society which does take some care for the weak in its midst can still be systematically unjust to other classes or races, thought of as so different that they somehow need not be considered as fellow human beings at all. North America is guilty of this kind of discrimination at numerous points; in the treatment of the North American Indian, the Negro, migrant workers, and overseas peoples whose immigration is not permitted.

The Christian commitment to the neighbor is not even limited to the stranger; it extends as well to the enemy. Not only those whom our society does not treat fairly, but even those whom, with apparent good reason and a good conscience, it treats definitely as adversaries are to be the objects of Christian concern. A Christian witness should represent the claims and the needs of the absent; all those whose interests seem genuinely opposed to those of one's own nation or society. Again, such concern for the "enemy" should not mean blindness to his own weaknesses and faults; but Christians should be more concerned and more capable than others for giving the "other side" a hearing.

G. When we concede that the state cannot be expected to trust the Holy Spirit, as when the Anabaptists and the Quaker theologian Robert Barclay agreed that the magistrates cannot be expected to be nonresistant, this does not mean that we shall ever completely accept specific governmental violences in the way in which socially conservative Christianity has usually done. The acceptance of the state which we associate with classical Lutheranism resulted generally in the government's taking the least idealistic and least progressive of the available alternatives; a realistic Christian social critique will always require the highest attainable aim. We do not ask of the government that it be nonresistant; we do, however, ask that it take the most just and the least violent action possible. For the state to take this least evil path would, in fact, in spite of what we have said above, call for a certain kind of faith. For an army to respect the prescriptions of the Geneva Convention regarding the treatment of prisoners when the enemy does not means for the military leader the acceptance of a practical disadvantage. Not to respect these standards undermines the moral validity of the military cause; to respect them means running a risk. For a government to abandon recourse to the death penalty, for a government in power to permit free elections, for a candidate for election to renounce fraudulent methods when he knows the adversary is using them, for a powerful nation to submit to the "rule of law," will always call for some sort of faith; i.e., a willingness to sacrifice immediate selfish ends for the sake of principle. At this one point liberal pacifism was basically right. It called the nation to an act of faith. It was wrong when the act of faith was called for in such idealistic terms as to be inconceivable for the state. It was however right in the insight that nothing just is ever cheap. The choice between violence, which is always the easiest way, and justice, which is more difficult, more dangerous, and superficially less efficacious, is always a question of faith.

H. The efforts of some to provide their rule with greater moral strength have coincided with the efforts of others to criticize their rulers more effectively, to create the concept of *legitimacy* or authority exercised *de jure*. The *de jure* character of a given government may be measured by quite varied criteria: by legitimate succession, as in monarchic dynasties, by the consent of the governed, as in the constitution of Western democracies, or by standards applied to the actual functioning of a government. Some would judge by whether the state makes for itself absolute or religious claims, such as were responsible for Christians' resistance to Adolf Hitler; others would judge by the legality of its practices (fraud, racism, constitutionality). Often today the recognition of a given regime is dependent on its position between the power blocs, independently both of how it came to be and of how it behaves. This does not necessarily mean that the two major powers actually make every such decision on a basis of crass partisanship; it is rather their convinced belief that only a government after their own pattern can be truly democratic or free. For the Marxist, only a government receiving its orders from a highly organized worker's party is truly a legitimate and free government. For the West, only a government constituted by free elections is valid, which means, in effect, the maintenance of social control by the existing feudal rulers in many parts of the world. Only one of the criteria mentioned above, namely that of direct juridical or personal succession from an earlier leader, is objective and clear. Governments in exile live from this claim; but they live only as long as they find powerful friends. Applied strictly, this criterion would disqualify everyone; for there is no regime whose beginning was not either revolution or conquest.

The logical implication of any concept of legitimacy — its *raison d'etre,* in fact—is the point where a given state may be declared *not* to be legitimate and its removal by war or revolution thereby justified.[8] It is just this conclusion that Jesus countered as He rejected Zealotism and that Paul opposes in Romans 13. It is the powers that *be* to which we ought to be subjected under God for the sake of conscience.

Yet it should not be thought that such concepts as orderly succession and the consent of the governed thereby become useless. Not only do they remain highly effective tools for criticizing an existing regime; it is furthermore often the case that we are called to be subjects not to one ruler but to two, a fact which many theological discussions of the authority of the state fail to note. Prince versus emperor, state or province versus federal government, bureaucracy versus constitution, executive versus judiciary, revolutionary underground versus colonial occupation; Katanga versus Congo—repeatedly the choice is not between subjection and rebellion as two possible attitudes toward the same government,

8 This is the argument used by Karl Barth against Hitler. Nazism was a non-state, an anti-state. The cause of the state properly so-called would be served by removing Hitler. This line of thought in Reformed circles goes all the way back to the Huguenots.

but between two "lords" competing for recognition and support. The subjects themselves, and sometimes other parties as well, may then have to make decisions on some ground other than the *de facto* exercise of sovereignty since this is divided. Here legitimacy may well be the key. When, for instance, in the late 1950s and early 1960s in the American South state law and the rulings of the United States Supreme Court stood in direct contradiction to one another, Christians had to decide which of these sovereignties was the most legitimate. Whether this decision was made on the basis of a prior ideological commitment to state rights or on weighing which way of dealing with the Negro problem was actually the right one, the decision reached was an application of one form or another of the concept of legitimacy and thereby a witness to both governments.

⟨ I ⟩ The ethical dilemma of the statesman is commonly defined in terms of possible alternate choices and their calculable results. Whether to arm, to stop nuclear tests, to recognize China's existence, or to suspend capital punishment is decided on the basis of expected results. The fact is, however, that results are not calculable. The situation is never fully known nor fully under control, and the effect of every choice will be different from what is expected. Reinhold Niebuhr has analyzed in great detail this phenomenon which he calls "irony," where idealism and pragmatism alike produce political results far from those intended.[9] George F. Kennan, who has similarly described this phenomenon in numerous case studies, concludes that the argument for political strategies chosen pragmatically with a view to obtaining defined immediate goals is seriously undermined by this observation. He concludes that concern for proper procedure (honesty, due process of law, constitutionality) and for fundamental moral principles should remain paramount in short-term decisions and will in the long run be the most effective.[10] Most discussion of political problems, especially in the field of armaments, has not yet clearly faced the truth that the degree of predictive accuracy is not attainable which would be necessary to justify making decisions on the basis of expected results. This observation confirms indirectly the Bible's assumption that we cannot calculate how obedience and success are connected, even though in the long run the right way is also the most effective. The good action is measured by its conformity to the command and to the nature of God and not by its success in achieving specific results.

9 Reinhold Niebuhr, *The Irony of American History*, Scribner, 1952.
10 George F. Kennan, "Foreign Policy and Christian Conscience," *Atlantic*, May 1959, p. 44. Herbert Butterfield also has written (*Christianity and History*, Bell/London, 1959, pp. 93 ff.) of the folly of basing decisions on predictable results, when the very fact that millions of other parties are simultaneously and independently doing the same thing makes it a mathematical certainty that the world in which I must carry out my decision will not be the one on the basis of which it was made.

6. EXAMPLES OF
POLITICAL JUDGMENT

IN THE ACTION OF THE Christian social analyst, attempting to apply his middle axioms to the changing contemporary scene, we shall expect that his judgments will usually coincide with the best informed secular analysis. The samples chosen below are therefore not meant as the advocacy of anything novel, but rather as demonstrating that we can explain theologically evaluations which by and large are confirmed by the most objective of those who analyze similar problems on common-sense grounds. Since these samples are intended as demonstrations of a logical procedure and not as full-fledged discussions in their own right, the validity of the case made above for a Christian social critique does not stand or fall with one's agreement with the positions that now will be suggested.

A. *International Conflict*

Christian realism about the nature of man and the state will first of all insist on the impossibility of the "crusade." Never is the political situation such that all the right is on one side; no political goal is so desirable as to justify the indiscriminate use of all available means of coercion. It may well be that in some respects the institutions and political traditions on one side of the iron curtain are a lighter gray than those of the other bloc; the difference is never between black and white. For this reason the interest of peace is not best served by the domination of the world even by an utterly benevolent nation, such as each of the major contenders in our day pretends to be, but rather by a controlled balance of power. The inadequate awareness of human sinfulness which justifies the "crusade" mentality, in the end means both too much government (unchallenged domination, with all the room it gives for the play of human pride and power hunger) and too little (the ultimate dis-order which is war).

The error involved in considering one's own nation or bloc to be utterly benevolent and the adversary utterly evil is compounded by every effort to undergird such a claim with appeals to a higher moral authority, to the rule of law, or even to Christian values. Such an appeal injects a further dimension of pride and further hinders a sane judgment of the realities with which politics must deal. A case in point is the refusal on the part of American governments to concede the existence of the continental Chinese government, in the thought that a government should be recognized only if it has proved that it will "be good." The claim that the

Chiang regime is the legitimate government of all continental China and therefore entitled to United Nations representation as a major power is a further confusion of moralism and realism which can only lead away from the peace which government is supposed to guarantee.

It would be possible to argue that the *de jure* recognition of governments—or at least membership in the United Nations, which is another question— should be limited to the nations which merit it through a degree of constitutionality, stability, respect for human rights, faithfulness to commitments. Such a suggestion might have some merit if it were applied consistently, and if the specific function of the club of relatively good nations were defined; but arguing from here to the nonexistence of some regime—or even to the necessity of destroying a given regime, such as that of Castro— is quite another matter.

B. *International Government*

Just as within an established government we have distinguished between the function of holding violence to a minimum and the intention to establish an ideal society, so also in the international realm experience has sufficiently indicated that the United Nations is best understood as an improvement on traditional means of carrying on the never-ending shifting and balancing of pressures which is the task of diplomacy. Neither Woodrow Wilson's hope for a society of nations endowed with effective sanctions or Franklin Roosevelt's dream of maintaining the wartime unity of the Allied Powers has been practical. The desirability of one central world government with unchallengeable coercive powers is open to serious question; not because world order is a bad thing, but precisely because the best way to have order is not to establish one governmental authority with no counterbalances capable of limiting it. True international unity will grow best through the imponderable contributions of labor, food, health, postal, and other such collaboration where the sanctions of police violence are not constantly just below the surface.

This caution should apply to those who place utopian hopes in the United Nations or in World Federation as a cure for the world's needs. In reality a society of nations with effective sovereignty is like anarchy; it is a dream. A much more limited United Nations organization, like the one we now have, in spite of—or rather thanks to—the very limited and modest character of the claims it can make, is preferable to what we would have without it.

We should further be reminded that as long as an international agency uses war as if it were police action, it is not a simple extension of the state of Romans 13 to the international level. Even the smallest and most gentlemanly war strikes more innocent than guilty persons. For an international system of courts and coercion to be truly spoken of as *police*, ways would have to be found to make its sanctions apply to responsible individuals on the basis of clearly defined crimes, with individual nations not promising to accept punishment as a nation but agreeing to extradite any offender, even political leaders, for trial and eventual punishment. Defining effective international government in this way is of course setting an idealistic goal; but it is less idealistic than the idea that military action could be truly an instrument of justice.

C. International Law

Every nation attempts to explain the justification for its military actions by appeal to some sort of moral law. The temptation for "Christian" nations to conceive of themselves as agents of God's wrath is especially strong. This is to forget that the "agent of God's wrath" is not thereby doing a just deed. God in no way approved of the aggressive tyranny of Assyria (Isaiah 10), though He used and channeled it. It cannot be argued that there exists a clearly defined and knowable system of natural law for states to justify their violence (Where would we go to find it?'). The middle axioms for evaluating international affairs are deduced not positively from some vision of universal moral law, but negatively from a case-by-case awareness of specific abuses which call for correction. For example: the rights of self-determination and political independence for all peoples are not natural obligations, for nothing in natural law decides on what level self-determination should take place. Should the continent, the nation, or the village do the voting? No one has advocated self-determination for Goa as over against either India or Portugal, or for Taiwan as against either of the Chinese governments. Nor has there been since 1865 much serious argument that the unity of the U.S.A. is immoral because it was founded on the violent repression of an independence movement. The concept of the right of self-determination retains a very real value in the negative sense; in that there is no excuse for imperial domination of any people which is capable and desirous of governing itself. Yet the nation continues to be an arbitrary creature of circumstance, and no system of law that takes the nation to be a juridical and moral absolute can be realistic. There exists no unity called Indochina which it is a sin to partition; even the unity of Korea, which was far older, was no absolute that could justify the drive to the Yalu by which the United Nations-United States forces discarded the police character of the initial military action and brought China openly into the Korean War.

47

Thus, though speaking of rights when such concepts are effective instruments of communication, the Christian critique of political affairs will continue to think less of general obligations than of specific injustices which visibly disserve the harmony and unity of society.

D. The Ethics of War

Our general thesis has been that the policing function of the state is to a degree legitimate and that war is illegitimate, for the clear reason that the police function can fit the prescriptions of Romans 13 and 1 Timothy 2; it can distinguish the innocent from the guilty and can preserve a semblance of order, whereas war cannot. This, however, does not mean that the church has nothing to say as to the conduct of war. The continuum of increasing tolerability, leading from total disorder to the kingdom of God, can be spoken to by the church at any point, in terms of the choice between greater and lesser evils available at that point. When the church's testimony against war has not been heard, the church does not therefore become silent or irrelevant; she still has a word about the ways of waging war.

Once hostilities have broken out choices constantly remain to be made between approximations of the police concept which will aim at correcting a particular injustice with the hope of ending hostilities as soon as possible by obliging the offender to concede the point, and on the other hand the crusade concept, as it was crystallized by Franklin D. Roosevelt in the slogan "unconditional surrender," aiming not at setting right a particular iniquity but at eliminating the enemy. This latter concept destroys the fabric of society to a degree far graver than the original offense and therefore creates more problems than it resolves. The former police conception of limited war, while not intrinsically legitimate, is at least amenable to certain controls and capable of being worked progressively into a system of international conventions and agencies of mediation, as the crusade is not. The unconditional surrender mentality contributed in a major way to the present East-West problem by creating a power vacuum in central Europe and favoring a too unqualified alliance of the Western Powers with the U.S.S.R. before 1945. In the same way, the systematic anti-Communism of the Western states since 1950, accepting any kind of alliance even with dictators and feudal tyrants, is equally unwholesome.

A corollary of this observation is the distinction between military and political objectives. If the extermination of the enemy is the goal, then any method, any cost, and any alliance will be justified. If, on the other hand, there is a defined war aim which can make some claim to be just, then some methods, some weapons, and some alliances, even though militarily necessary, will be excluded. The relinquishing of East Germany and the Balkans to Communism, and the concessions at Yalta to bring Russia unnecessarily into the Pacific War were fruits of such a domination of policy by strategy.[1]

A still clearer example of the wrongness of crusade warfare is the case of the atomic bombing of Japan, which had sued for peace before the bombs were used.[2] The bombs were in no sense necessary to win the war but only to make the surrender unconditional, and represented a serious moral defeat for the Western world.

E. The Just War

We have seen that certain concepts, such as that of the lesser evil, while illegitimate for guiding Christian discipleship, are still relevant in the elaboration of an ethic for the state. The same can be said for the traditional Catholic doctrine of the just war. That all means of nonmilitary settlement of conflicts must have been exhausted, that the harm done must be less than the offense to be corrected or hindered, that the resulting order must be more stable than the previous one, that the aims of war must be defined so that the enemy knows on what terms he may have peace, that there must be sufficient strength so that there is a preponderant probability of victory, that the cause must be clearly not self-aggrandizement, that the hostilities must be undertaken by a legitimate government—all such criteria are useful attempts to delimit, in terms of the function of the state, the cases in which the use of violence is the least illegitimate. That there can be a just war in the Christian sense of the word *just* or *righteous* is, of course, excluded by definition; we can make the point only negatively. When the conditions traditionally posed for a just war are *not* fulfilled, then a war is unjust to the point that even a state, resolved to use violence, is out of order in its prosecution. This is the basis of our condemnation of the atomic bomb *even for the warring state.*

F. The Penalty of Death

Jean Lasserre, whose *War and the Gospel* is the most adequate theological presentation of Christian pacifism, holds that the good which governments should serve (Romans 13:4) is defined by the Decalog, and that therefore even the state, though it may use force, should not take life.[3] Lasserre's analysis of *Romans* 13 and

---

1 Hanson Baldwin, "Churchill Was Right," *Atlantic Monthly,* July 1954, pp. 23 ff.
2 Robert C. Batchelder, *The Irreversible Decision,* 1939-1950, Houghton-Mifflin, 1962; for Japanese desire for a negotiated peace, cf. pp. 83 ff.
3 Lasserre, *op. cit.;* see pp. 145 ff. for the discussion of the Decalog, one of the most original portions of the book; pp. 180 ff. concerning the death penalty. Our own argument against capital punishment was cited above, Chap. 5, Note 6.

John 8 in this respect is excellent. It may, however, be objected that Lasserre is here thinking of a proper order or natural law, defining on the basis of a particular text (the Ten Commandments) the task of the state. This would seem too unparadoxical. In the hypothetical ideal state there would, of course, be no capital punishment because there would be no crime. In a society sufficiently influenced by Christian witnessing that other more offensive and more corrigible forms of lethal violence have been largely eliminated, to have policemen unarmed and to abolish capital punishment is an intelligent and available possibility because it is within reach. In a society—such as those of the Middle East, for example —which has no due process of law, to begin by attacking the legislative provision for the death penalty would be to raise the wrong issue first. This does not mean that capital punishment is ever justified; there may, however, be times when it is not the most offensive of the unjustified things which the state is doing.

G. Revolution

Classical scholastic ethics always devoted a chapter to the possibility of resisting or even assassinating a tyrant. As far as the Christian is concerned, the way Jesus behaved under Pilate, who was the unjust representative of a totalitarian occupying power, makes clear that even unjust rule is to be accepted and resistance to it expressed only in a Christian way. The teaching of Paul in Romans 13 makes the same point.[4] On the political level it, however, still would be arguable that resistance to and even the possible unseating of an unjust ruler could be justified as politically legitimate. The conditions under which this could take place would be that the methods of revolution would be less violent than the tyrant's present way of ruling, and the preponderant probability that the order which would follow the revolution would be more just, orderly, and peaceful than that which preceded. In such a case, the change of regimes may itself be the established order which will best keep the peace. The more centralized and totalitarian a government is, the more possibility there is that a *coup d'etat* could fulfill these conditions; the more a government is decentralized and democratic the less chance there is that such a method would be needed or that it would work. A violent revolution which destroys the entire governmental structure could in any case not be justified, since, like war, it sacrifices the very fabric of human coexistence.

4 Almost alone among conservative evangelical theologians, whose patriotism is generally less carefully qualified, the late Donald Gray Barnhouse has recognized in his commentary on Romans 13 that a faithful interpretation of the passage would condemn the American Revolution.

H. Nuclear Pacifism

It is common knowledge that an almost immeasurable increase in the destructive capacity of modern weapons has led many who are not convinced in principle that killing is wrong to conclude, nevertheless, that warfare in which modern nuclear, chemical, or bacterial weapons would be used is not permissible morally either for the Christian or for the state. This "nuclear pacifism" has found significant expressions among West German Protestant theologians, within Roman Catholicism, within a study commission of the World Council of Churches, and also among American literary and scientific groups whose moral motivation is not exclusively Christian.[5] Christian pacifists are faced with the new challenge of having to decide whether to make common cause with nuclear pacifism in their testimony to the state. There would be several reasons for such an alliance, the first among them being the defense of peace against the threat involved in the continued nuclear weapon stockpiling. Furthermore, by using the argument that the situation is changed, it might be possible to lead to an effective practical pacifism in the present those fellow-Christians who would not be ready to re-examine their action in the past.

In order seriously to evaluate this new development, we must recognize that it is composed of several different elements. First of all, the entire case may be based on the belief that war has entered a new dimension; that weapons are not only quantitatively larger but qualitatively of a different type. One reason for holding to this is that the genetic effects of fallout, or the possibility of completely depopulating a large portion of the globe, including even plant life, involve a disruption of creation itself. It is indisputable that the new weapons do have this characteristic in a greater degree than earlier methods of warfare. From a Christian viewpoint it is, however, hard to see why a war which menaces creation is fundamentally worse than all other wars, which have always menaced redemption.

It may be from another perspective that the new dimension in nuclear warfare consists simply in the fact that the size of the destructive effect removes the new weapons from all pretense of controllability and aimability which could be applied to conventional weapons. This difference is a matter of degree, and with the de-

---

5 Probably the most significantly new statement to come from a church of the *Volkskirche* tradition is *Het Vraagstak van de Kernwapenen* (1962), a statement of the Reformed Church of the Netherlands, which categorically condemns nuclear weapons as not legitimately usable for any conceivable purpose. The tentative study report of a World Council of Churches Study Commission which the WCC, after emphatically declaring the study to be incomplete, dissolved in midstream, rejects imprecisely the use of nuclear arms in all-out war. Cf. R. Billheimer and T. Taylor, "Christians and the Prevention of War in an Atomic Age," SCM Press, 1961, pp. 36 ff.

velopment of smaller tactical atomic bombs, the gap between nuclear weapons and the blockbusters of World War II is constantly decreasing. Similarly, the widespread idea that modern conventional or atomic war is qualitatively different from the wars of the Middle Ages is open to considerable challenge as far as the human significance of its destruction is concerned. A prolonged period of hostilities like the Thirty Years' War could devastate a whole province and render it unproductive for a generation just as effectively as this was done at Verdun in the first world war or in some German cities in the second, or even in Hiroshima.

In still another direction, the case may be made that the use of nuclear weapons would be suicidal. This argument has certainly a great pragmatic weight, but for Christian ethics it makes less difference. Unless war is wrong in the first place, the fact that it is costly to him who resorts to it only invests the suicide with the halo of martyrdom (as has already been suggested by some politically conservative German theologians and some patriotic American fundamentalists).

With the "atomic stalemate" or "balance of horror," which some hope will prevent the outbreak of a major war, the likelihood of local non-nuclear wars is, in fact, increased, it being the only nonsuicidal way either political bloc will have to strengthen or defend its position. At the very best, such "brush-fire" wars will pose all the moral problems of conventional war; conscientious objection on a personal level will continue to be relevant. In all probability, however, the pressures of enemy tactics will force the use of methods (torture, brainwashing, reprisals, summary execution of prisoners, gas, napalm, and bacterial weapons) which are just as definitely new dimensions violating pre-nuclear military ethics as is the bomb itself. Exclusive preoccupation with the nuclear issue tends to hide this fact, which actually should be a far more live issue since offenses of this kind are continuing to occur, whereas the hazard of nuclear warfare is only potential.[6]

The first responsibility of the Christian and the church remains obedience at the level where live options exist. Conscientious objection therefore remains a significant issue, over against the arguments of those who have said that today the *only* question is how to prevent the outbreak of nuclear war. It is now clear that a nuclear war would be over before land armies could function, to say nothing of the draft; in that sense conscientious objection no

6 The most rigorous and extensive effort to apply traditional "just-war" theory to the nuclear age, Paul Ramsey's *Modern War and Christian Conscience* (Duke University Press, 1961), while going to great lengths to respect the immunity of noncombatants in a hypothetical nuclear conflict, gives no counsel about applying the same criteria—to say nothing of the other classical requirements—to the kind of wars actually fought since 1945 in Viet Nam, Hungary, Algeria, or Angola.

longer relates to participation in war itself. But the claim of the objector has never been essentially that by his refusal to serve he would prevent war, or that what he wished to avoid was just the fighting. Technical change has made conscientious objection irrelevant only in the sense that it has also made military service irrelevant. It remains essential, though not sufficient, as a testimony to the abiding priority of simple personal obedience over calculations of effectiveness.

Chemical and bacteriological weapons, although not used in World War II, continue to be produced and stockpiled. Their use in future major war may be more likely now than that of the bomb and constitutes just as serious a worsening of war's effects as would thermonuclear weapons. This is another issue which concentration on nuclear pacifism can obscure. It therefore would seem that there are no adequate grounds for holding that the moral issue facing pacifism has changed qualitatively. This, however, does not necessarily mean that the growing interest in nuclear pacifism should be ignored or minimized. A quantitative difference is still a significant difference, especially as concerns our witness to society. In such a witness to the realm of moral relativity we may always seek tactical alliances on particular issues with those who do not share all of our basic convictions, insofar as such collaboration involves no ultimate dishonesty. When nonpacifists become relative pacifists, it cannot be the desire of pacifists to rub it in that "we were right" before and "they were wrong." Such considerations of right and wrong are not insignificant academically, as far as the intrinsic logic of our arguments in the past was concerned, but to make this point is not Christianly useful in most contexts. The possibility of making common cause with other antimilitarists is even more clear for nuclear testing, with its raising of general radioactivity levels through fallout. Since the military utility of most testing is open to serious challenge, and since the deleterious effects both on health and on foreign policy are real and present, not only potential, and strike innocent persons and nations with no stake in American or Canadian national defense, the case for outlawing nuclear testing should be valid for a sufficiently large circle of concerned persons to be an immediately relevant political option.

I. Radical Pacifism

A most extreme form of what we refer to above as "conscientious non-cooperation" is the realm of possible forms of objection usually classified as "radical pacifism." This title is itself an adequately precise one only for those who reject sweepingly all it refers to as incompatible with the Christian desire for orderly government or with the Christian's subjection to government. Even the attempted subdivisions suggested here are not sufficiently exhaustive.

53

a. It is possible to use civil disobedience, practiced without violence but in intentional opposition to a legal authority, in order to lead toward the acceptance of certain policy changes on the part of government by causing loss or embarrassment to those in authority, or by disrupting the economy. This kind of method has been suggested as feasible for large groups of people, in fact, as a most effective tool of social conflict and coercion.[7] Such "direct action," as it is often called, is, in fact, an intentional involvement in the power struggle rather than a witness to those in power from the perspective of a minority Christian commitment. It may very well be that the claims of the nonviolent revolutionary group are, on the level of moral or democratic legitimacy (above p. 40), more just than those of the other claimants to power, so that the Christian could speak to this agency of power as well as to the currently dominant government; the nonviolent direct actionists, however, are not themselves predominantly interested in speaking to those in power but rather in wielding power themselves in the interest of justice.

b. The withdrawal of cooperation with government may be meant as an act of moral disengagement, symbolizing, and in the minds of some perhaps attaining, a real degree of moral purity through noninvolvement. This is the rationale which leads some to avoid income tax payments by living on an economic level under the deduction threshold. It is also the rationale behind the conviction of some nonresistant Christians who do not vote because they feel that to exercise the franchise is to share moral responsibility for all the actions of government.

c. The act of civil disobedience may be understood as a symbolic and dramatic gesture, bearing no immediate causal relation to the processes of government, with which it does not directly interfere, and of no direct and self-evident moral significance. In this category we find acts of trespassing on missile bases, sailing a vessel into parts of the Pacific reserved for atomic tests, holding forbidden meetings or demonstrations, disregarding segregation in transportation facilities.

d. Other actions of this same demonstrative character may be completely legal; marches, vigils, fasts.

We would misunderstand if we analyzed these latter two demonstrative types of witness by asking either whether they are politically effective or whether the particular point at which their choice was made to disobey or to demonstrate was a simple and evident matter

---

7 The clearest testimony to this conception of nonviolence as a tool of coercion is the title of Richard B. Gregg's *War Without Violence*. It is doubtful that Gandhi's own conception was this pragmatic. Reinhold Niebuhr also advocates nonviolence, not as uniquely loving or pure, but because in some contexts it is the best kind of force. *Moral Man and Immoral Society*, Scribners 1932, pp. 246-51.

of right. The justification for these efforts is a symbolic one; they seek to arouse public opinion to the depth of a moral challenge which has been hidden or underestimated; they may seek especially to catch the attention and appeal to the moral sense of men in power to make them more aware of the inhumanity of their action. It is by this intention that they should be measured; is the point they seek to make clearly made? is it presented to the proper persons? does it formulate a moral challenge to which someone in particular can conceivably respond?

The neatness of the above fourfold classification is logical but deceptive. For almost necessarily, the various aspects will be found coinciding. The dramatic gesture, whether illegal (c) or legal (d), will only be communicative if there is about it at the same time an appearance of moral appropriateness (b). The moral withdrawal (b) is self-deceptive and even pharisaical if it is thought to be morally adequate; the picture changes, however, if it takes on the dramatic dimension (c or d), or changes in another direction if it becomes coercive (a).

Our present assignment is to survey this entire realm only under the heading of "witness." In situations where more normal channels of address to persons in authority are not available, either because (as in modern America) the actual decision makers are behind a screen of bureaucracy and all communication is vitiated by the mass media, or (as in Gandhi's India) because of nondemocratic forms of government, such approaches may be the most proper ones available. Their adequacy depends to a great extent on factors that cannot be rationally evaluated; whether a given symbolic gesture will communicate at all and just what needs to be said are probably a matter more of artistic than of logical sensitivity. This witness will be most forceful if it coincides with a clear prior moral commitment rather than being a mere protest. It will be most effective if some alternative action is actually proposed; if the intention is not to embarrass an adversary but to create a climate in which he may find himself more free to do right; and if the gesture is directed to persons who have some discretionary responsibility so that they can do something about the challenge placed before them. From the perspective of this present study, these efforts will be most appropriate when it is most possible to distinguish between their witness function and a self-seeking participation in the power struggle. The difficulty of making this distinction, however, cannot justify avoiding such channels of witness entirely.

J. Involvement in Political Responsibility

This entire treatment has intentionally avoided the question, though it is closely related to it, of directly responsible involvement in the functioning of the state. Here we think not primarily of such state-supported functions as public school teaching or forestry or even of legislative functions, but of the police-type activity which we have seen to be most characteristic of the state. If it is granted that nonresistant love is the way of the disciple, and if it is said at the same time that police force, within definite limits, is legitimate in the fallen world, can the Christian be the policeman?

In the past, every party to this discussion has rapidly concluded that the answer is negative. Some have drawn this conclusion because they believe in it for themselves. Others have used it to demonstrate that the nonresistant position is ultimately impossible because it is socially irresponsible. That such a conclusion is the most normal one can hardly be contested. Here our concern is to move behind the self-evident to check whether this hasty conclusion calls for shadings or qualifications.

The answer of the pre-Constantinian church was negative; the Christian as an agent of God for reconciliation has other things to do than to be in police service. Even the decent heathen were capable of administering decent justice under Rome, and even when the administration of justice was unfaithful, Christians saw their task as one of patient suffering, not taking over themselves the work of the police. We should, however, note that this negative attitude toward government functions had its roots *not* in a moral absolutism and the search for complete abstention from any use of force and any relation to government, but rather in considerations of relative importance and urgency, and (in an accessory way) in the state's idolatry.

The post-Constantinian church obviously accepted government service by Christians, but for reasons which cannot be deemed adequate. (The reasons given then were by no means as serious as Niebuhr's.) Our minds should remain open to the possible rational or biblical arguments of those who might claim that the attainment of a privileged social position by the church in the fourth century called for changes in morals, ecclesiology, and eschatology; thus far it must be admitted that clear and cogent arguments for this have not been brought. The church's compromise with the world, to which we habitually attach the label *Constantinian* although Constantine himself was not to blame for it and the change was not complete until Theodosius and Augustine, was taken for granted and presupposed, rather than being carefully weighed and argued through.

The question, May a Christian be a policeman? is posed in legalistic terms. The answer is to pose the question on the Christian level: Is the Christian *called* to be a policeman? We know he is called to be an agent of reconciliation. Does that general call, valid for every Christian, take for certain individuals a form of a specific call to be also an agent of the wrath of God? Stating the question in this form makes it clear that if the Christian can by any stretch of the imagination find his calling in the exercise of state-commanded violence, he must bring us (i.e., lay before the brother-hood) the evidence that he has such a special calling. Long enough we have been told that the position of the conscientious objector is a prophetic one, legitimate but only for the specially called few; in truth we must hold that the nonresistant position is the normal and normative position for every Christian, and it is the use of violence, even at that point where the state may with some legitimacy be violent, that requires an exceptional justification. This writer has met no one testifying to such an exceptional call.[8] Generally those who seek political positions do not admit a need to justify their actions as discipleship, within the framework defined by a prior admission of the nonresistant teaching of the New Testament.[9]

Between the position of the "witness" speaking to the statesman from within the church and the hypothetical extreme of a Christian wielding the sword of justice within legal limits, there runs the great gamut of degrees of involvement or participation, where most actual decisions lie. The present paper is not aimed at this problem, since its concern is for the areas where the Christian's witness goes further than his action can conscientiously follow. Yet it may also bear fruit for the problem of Christian involvement:

a) by freeing us from feeling that we must always choose between faithful but irrelevant dualism and relevant but unfaithful compromise. From this sterile dilemma the New Testament's view of a dualism of relevance frees us.

b) by teaching us not to ask about compromising on absolutes, but rather to seek for the points along the continuum between tyranny and the Kingdom where significant differences of degree may be pegged.

c) by disassociating *involvement* from *moralism*. The incarnation is by definition *involvement;* Christ himself was in the middle of the socio-political maelstrom of military occupation and underground war, "yet without sin." To equate *involvement* with *compromise* and then *compromise* with *sin* so that sin is an *essential*

---

8 Gordon Kaufman, who, as a way of making a point about the structure of ethics has suggested such a possibility (Cf. above, Chap. 3, Note 7), does not personally testify to such leading.

9 Habitually, the issue at stake here is phrased as if the Christian were offered political power and needed to choose between accepting and refusing it. This is never the case except in hereditary monarchies, and then only for one person. The real option, whether in democracy or elsewhere, is not whether to *accept* power, but whether to *seek* it. To enter into this struggle and to win it normally will pose other moral challenges far more grave than are involved in the office-holder's share of responsibility for the police.

dimension of the human situation is not only Christologically un-orthodox and the death of further fruitful thought; it sells out in advance to the same kind of legalism it intended to combat, for it defines *sin* as the breaking of absolute rules.

K. *The Economic Order*

The most current modern use of the term *prophetic witness* is coupled in the minds of many with leanings toward socialism and the planned economy which were characteristic of theological liberalism and which survive to some extent in specialized church agencies for social concerns. To this issue we can speak only very sketchily. The question we ask is not, What would be the ideal economic order? but, Under what conditions is the intervention of the state in economic matters justified? We are speaking of the state *as sword,* asking therefore not what social institutions are justified or desirable, but which institutions actually should be backed up by political sanctions and the ultimate appeal to vio-lence. It would follow from what has been said above about the state that measures of checking, control, and compensation, which seek to remedy specific iniquities and dangers, will be more in order than attempts to create out of nothing new economic systems. The actual socialization of certain elements in the economy may be dictated by considerations of justice, efficiency, risk, or public welfare—Tennessee Valley Authority, national parks, public schools, roads, post office, public health, etc.—where competition or un-supervised private management would be harmful to the general welfare; but socialism as a panacea and centralized planning as the major guide of economic development are open to challenge both theologically and practically. This observation does not rehabilitate *laissez-faire* capitalism nor condemn the concerns of the social gospel, nor does it deny that sometimes limited socialization may at times be the best way to avoid the use of monopoly by private interests. Intervention is most justified where the delinquency it aims to prevent or correct is the most directly harmful. When the state forces the Amish to send their children to school or accept social security, we cannot adequately evaluate this by making religious liberty an absolute, nor by discussing whether it would be good for everyone to have a certain amount of education and a certain retirement income; the question is how much harm will come to society if these laws are not thus violently and intransi-gently enforced. Where the state acts without direct sanctions, for instance, in running universities, the post office, and agricultural experimentation, it is acting as the agent of *voluntary* social co-operation and the problem of the sword does not arise. The same is true of those dimensions of the welfare state, participation in which is voluntary. Even here, there would still be reasons of a

58

pragmatic nature (bigness, the spoils system, waste, impersonality, and fraud) which would lead us to prefer keeping some voluntary forms of community under other leadership.

Lest it be thought that we are here espousing a particular Jeffersonian or libertarian political philosophy of minimum government, it should be pointed out that the issue at stake here is not the degree of social planning or economic integration, but whether such planning and integration should be a) conceived of as in itself a value toward which more personal values should be sacrificed, and b) so identified with the police arm of the state that it is implemented by the use of the sword and every dissent is equated with political rebellion. We are not arguing for minimum government so much as for sobriety, humility, legality, decentralization, and humane tolerance in the exercise of whatever tasks the government undertakes and, even more basically, for the distinction between those governmental functions which clearly have to do with the forceful curbing of definable evils and those in which the state is simply serving as the agent of society for coordinating a common effort.

Here as elsewhere the framing of a Christian social critique does not presuppose, either practically or logically, one set of (non-Christian) moral standards for non-Christian society. No tyrant can be so low on the scale of righteousness that the Christian could not appeal to him to do at least a little better; no "Christianized" society can be so transformed as not to need constant criticism. In the relevant alternatives which we hold before men of state to give body to our critique, none will be good in the Christian sense; they will only be less evil. The term *legitimate* expresses this kind of qualified acquiescence accorded to the less wrong. When, for instance, we say (above, page 45) that police activity is legitimate and war is illegitimate, even for nations, *legitimate* does not mean right and good; it points rather to the minimal level of wrong (i.e., of disconformity to Christ, our only standard of right and good) which is the best we can expect under the circumstances.

It should be recalled that we are here working with a definition of the state as *sword;* a definition that seizes at the center the ethical problem with which we began. Had we begun with the state as the sum of organized human community, or the state as social contract, the conclusions here might be different. The distinction between policing evils and coordinating social cooperation is not a theoretically clear one, but it becomes clear each time we ask how the sanctions of the sword are involved.

7. THE CLASSICAL OPTIONS GRAPHICALLY PORTRAYED

EVER SINCE CHRISTIANITY CEASED to be the faith of a persecuted minority and there were found within the churches persons carrying responsibility for the state, Christian thinkers have been haunted by the intellectual problem of relating the needs of statesmanship to the standards of the gospel. As a result of numerous attempts to discuss what has been variously referred to as "the problem of compromise" or "the problem of responsibility," it seems clear that the discussion is so strongly dominated by a variety of historical ways of thinking about these problems that one can hardly make a new start without dealing directly with some of the major historical options. Whether right or wrong, they have determined the vocabulary and the understanding of the nature of the problem which continue to dominate the discussion. The graphic demonstration of some of these classical solutions which is here offered does not claim to be more than a caricature. The purpose is not to represent with accurate detail the positions of certain individuals or churches so much as to see in them types, each of which illustrates a general approach even if it is not historically true to the complexity of the positions taken by the persons or movements named. There is nothing particularly original about this typological approach, nor about the particular observations being made; the reason for surveying this history is to relate the solution being proposed here to the other traditional approaches.

A. The Medieval View

The understanding typologically attributed to classical Roman Catholic thought is that of the double standard. This approach can well be portrayed by the identification of two separate levels of moral demand. Whereas in Catholicism these two levels would apply in every significant realm of ethics, we are concerned especially with the problems of evil, retribution, and forgiveness, and can therefore represent these positions on a scale of differing degrees of retribution or forgiveness. In the center of the scale is the level of justice, where retribution and offense are exactly proportionate ("eye for eye, tooth for tooth"). Considerably below this would be the incommensurate vengeance exercised by a Lamech (Genesis 4:24). Above the level of equal retribution are rising degrees of willingness to forgive, the extreme being Jesus' instructions to forgive seventy times seven, i.e., to forgo retribution completely regardless of the measure of the offense. The lines marked on this graph stand for ethical norms. The graph does not show whether these standards are attainable or not; it is assumed that they are not intrinsically impossible of fulfillment.

For the major body of society, classical Roman Catholic moral theology thinks of certain basic precepts or commands which, if not identical with the level of exact retribution, remain quite close to that level, because of society's need for justice. What just behavior

MEDIEVAL

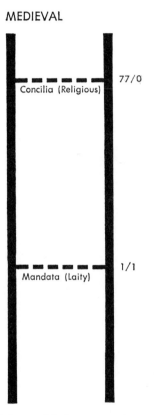

Concilia (Religious)   77/0

Mandata (Laity)   1/1

means on this level is knowable by reason to anyone, even a pagan, and Christian thought on the subject draws extensively from such men as Aristotle and Cicero.

Far above this is the ethical level of the evangelical councils, which are known only by special revelation and are really the norm only for very special Christians.

The difference between the two levels is a difference of vocation. Mankind is divided into two kinds of persons, the variations between them consisting precisely in the level of moral obligation on which they stand. Those who are truly saints belong with all of their life on the upper level; those who are responsible for the economic

61

and political function of the world may with no pangs of conscience remain on the other level, or rise above it only slightly; but for them to attempt to be saints would not only be unrealistic; it would be undesirable.

Let us look more in detail at the significance of the fact that the norm of justice is a definite quantity (i.e., a fixed point on the graph). Epistemologically, this presupposes that it is possible outside of the revelation of the incarnate Christ to know what justice is. It is further presupposed that we have standards to calculate what it means for the retribution to fit the offense (an eye for an eye, a tooth for a tooth; but how do we measure equivalence when the offense leaves the realm of anatomy?).

Since the norm of justice is both fixed and attainable, this means that we can conceive of, and perhaps with good coordination even achieve, a state which would be all that we could ask a state to be. Such a state would completely fulfill the requirements of justice, while making no attempt to act according to love. It would, in fact, not be good for a state having reached the level of justice to rise higher on the scale. For the state to move closer to forgiving love—e.g., by relaxing the application of the death penalty—would, in fact, not be truly higher, since it would mean the state's abandoning its own assignment of justice.

It goes without saying that on this basis it is possible to build a coherent social ethic, as Roman Catholicism has done with great clarity and thoroughness. That the norms of justice are knowable and distinct from redemptive love tends to presuppose that they are founded in creation, in the nature of man or society. It is this nature which will give us our guidance in knowing how to define not only retributive justice (which we are discussing on these graphs) but also attributive and distributive justice.

The awareness that the norms of justice are supposed to be founded in creation raises one serious weakness of this view, for we are discussing how justice can deal with evil. If, however, there is evil, we are no longer on the level of creation, but that of the Fall. Can we then know the norms of creation and of man's true nature? If we do know them, is it appropriate that we should use them as standards for guiding society after the Fall?

B. The Classical Lutheran View

It will be observed that this position is similar to the one analyzed above, in placing two distinct and definite lines on the graph. The standard of suffering, forgiving love, as revealed in Christ, is substantially the same; likewise the standard of justice. If anything, the distinctness and definiteness of the standards of justice are greater in Lutheranism than in Catholicism. For whereas Catholicism founded its doctrine of natural law in philosophical realism, so that in order to know what a man's nature is one analyzes the *concept* of man, Lutheranism spoke rather of "order of creation," which, it was practically assumed, could be observed by looking empirically at society, by observing what a prince or a banker is.

Lutheranism differs distinctly, however, in its understanding of how individual Christians relate to both of these standards. Instead of dividing mankind into two categories, some saints living in perfect love and the mass of common men operating on the level of justice, Luther places every man on both levels. As an individual,

LUTHERAN

involved in face-to-face relations with his neighbor, every Christian is to be nonresistant, bearing patiently every kind of evil treatment. Likewise, every man, when he functions with a view to his assignment ("vocation" or "station") in society, operates on the lower level. Thus, instead of asking, What kind of person am I? as was the case in Catholicism, the Christian will ask from case to case and moment to moment, On what level am I now operating, in my station or as an individual? The graph symbolizes this condition by placing the Christian in a position of tension between the two levels. We noted above that for Catholicism the fact that moral performance is demanded indicates that it is attainable. For Lutheranism this has changed completely, as far as the norm for perfect love is concerned. Man is always a sinner, even though justified. His inability ever to attain perfect love is not only a result of the fact that he has social obligations which call him to do justice, but is also an outworking of his corrupt will. With reference, however, to the maintenance of justice, the insight into human sinfulness does not lead to any doubts about whether the standards of justice defined for the statesman in his station can be attained; Lutheranism traditionally places considerable confidence in rulers.

C. Calvinist Theocracy

When we move to the position represented first of all by Ulrich Zwingli and finally incorporated in the reformed societies of Geneva

CALVINIST/PURITAN

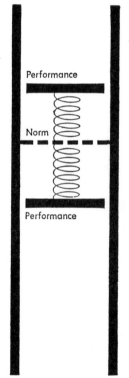

or the Netherlands, we find a series of very significant changes. First of all, the Reformed tradition is original in its rejection of any kind of dualism. No realm of life is removed from Divine

64

Sovereignty or from the moral norms imposed by revelation. Reason or nature cannot be the source of a different set of standards from those revealed in God's word. Insofar as reason and nature have any usefulness as concepts, they agree with the norms of revelation; they can never differ therefrom, as in the Catholic and Lutheran schemes. On the graph we therefore have only one norm line.

This line is not the level of pure justice, eye for eye retribution. The kings of the Old Testament are praised for their mercy and their care for widows and orphans. A puritan society in the Calvinist tradition is Christianized in a far-reaching way, with certain elements of New Testament ethics, such as the rejection of usury, built into the larger society. Thus the norm is above the level of pure justice. But neither is the line set on the level of *agape* love. The norm must be drawn from the whole Bible, including the Old Testament. It must serve as a standard for entire peoples, which are not yet in a position to take seriously a call to true self-sacrifice.

It would therefore be wrong even for individuals to attempt to function in a higher or more loving way, for they would then be unfaithful to their common responsibility for the civil order. For example, if a government is unjust, Christians are not to bear it as disciples of Christ, but to rebel; every individual is always responsible for the norms of order and it is never really loving for him to disobey them.

Although all men as individuals are sinners, an ideal theocracy is a possibility even in this world. It is, in fact, possible for a state to be too good—e.g., by laxity in the use of the death penalty or by disarming. The performance line (P) can fall either above or below the will of God for the state.

D. Liberal Pacifism

Standing in the Puritan-Nonconformist tradition, the liberal pacifist position tolerates no duality. There is only one norm, both for individuals and for societies; neither the Lutheran distinction between individual and social office nor the Catholic distinction between different kinds of people can be tolerated.

It is, however, not precisely definable just where the one line lies. Sometimes it is on the level of unretaliating forgiveness which we have called *agape*. Sometimes, however, it falls somewhat short of this, assuming that a certain residual necessary amount of justice can be maintained with a very redemptive approach. At still other times it goes even beyond *agape* in believing that suffering in itself may have a redemptive value. There is no clear distinction in the thought of liberal pacifism between these three upper levels, a fact which we have indicated by the slanting irregular line.

Since the norms for society and those for the individual coincide and are fixed on the high level of love, it is clear that justice and love are identical, as are reason and revelation. There are no problems that cannot be solved if we try hard and sin has not basically changed the original pattern of creation. Performance may actually fall somewhat short of the standards we hold before the state, but there is no reason that it needs to.

E. Reinhold Niebuhr

The contemporary thinker who has given the most careful attention to the subject we are dealing with is without doubt Reinhold Niebuhr. He begins by accepting major elements from all

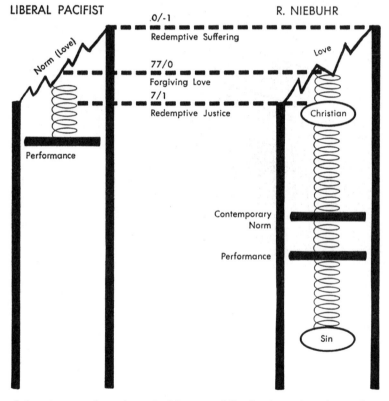

of the views we have been looking at. Like Lutheranism, he understands the individual Christian to be in a continuing tension between the ethical demands of two different levels. In face-to-face relations it is imperative and to some extent possible to follow the precepts of Christ; in social responsibility this is not only impossible but actually wrong because in the social dimension love expresses it-

66

self in the norms of responsibility, i.e., justice. Like Luther, he believes the decision in a specific situation will have to be made by the Christian on the basis of whether he finds himself in a purely personal relationship or in a context of responsibility; the choice between face-to-face and eye-for-eye depends on the presence or absence of the dimension of responsibility.

With the Catholic tradition, Niebuhr argues that there are certain ethical values in the Greco-Roman tradition, expressed most clearly in the pagan moralists of the classical age, which we need to add to Christianity in order to guide a responsible witness to the state or to a society at large. Thus the difference between uniquely Christian standards and those we apply to the state is not only that between pure idealism and compromise, but also between different sources of norms.

It is perhaps less broadly realized to what extent Reinhold Niebuhr is indebted for his analysis of this problem to continuing agreement with liberal pacifism. Like the liberal pacifist he used to be earlier, Niebuhr has only one real ideal, and that is the one at the top. There is no built-in justification for anything less than love. As with liberal pacifism, Niebuhr is not quite sure just where the ideal line runs. Sometimes, when arguing the inadequacy of *agape,* he seems to be equating it practically with absolute self-negation (the redemptive suffering beyond *agape*— symbolized on the graph by $0/-1$); at other times he thinks of pacifists as people who are trying to organize a redemptive but still somehow just and effective society $(7/1)$.

The originality of Niebuhr's position, which enables him to synthesize these otherwise irreconcilable views, is indicated on the graph by the fact that the "norm" line is not a fixed point. Although the demands of justice are distinct from those of love, they are not definite. We cannot find in natural law or elsewhere a clear definition of what the just state would be. In his own thinking probably Niebuhr's reason for this innovation is simply his experience in a study of the history of Christian thought and of social history. He has seen that justice is a relative and instrumental concept and not a fixed and clearly definable norm. Yet beyond this pragmatic discovery he has actually solved some of the problems raised by the other views. When justice was thought of as representing a fixed point on the scale, we had to ask how this point can be known and with what revelatory authority it is communicated to us. Niebuhr avoids these problems since the concept of justice which he will use at any given point is not a fixed quantity. This means that the justice line is double. Whereas in the earlier views the level of performance did not need to be indicated on the graph, since the norms by which we judge the state were not thought of as dependent upon what the state was doing, the actual performance level has to be indicated for Niebuhr because there is no other point of orientation. Thus we have an interplay of tensions such that the norm by which we speak to the state is always higher than present performance, but never so much higher as to be irrelevant.

Whereas in the earlier dualist systems the lower level was fixed by revelation, in Niebuhr's the only thing that holds down the set of tensions and norms is the weight of sin at the bottom. Sin is not an additional norm but a brute fact in the life of society. There is no philosophical reason for the state not to be loving; the only reason is factual.

Since the two justice lines are not fixed, it is an idle question to ask whether they are above or below the level of exact eye-for-eye equivalence. In fact this level of exact equivalence cannot and need not be known with real certainty. It may be spoken of hypothetically, as can other pagan ideas of justice, order, etc.; it is never a real norm either in value or in knowability. It is also an idle question to ask whether justice is attainable. At any given point, by the very nature of the situation shown graphically, the justice which it asks of the state is more than it is presently performing; yet in each case that which is asked is not impossible.

"Sectarian" Views

All of the positions analyzed thus far, conservative or liberal, old or new, pacifist or not, have one thing in common. They speak of the moral problem of an entire society without considering faith as a decisive dimension. They may distinguish between two kinds of Christians, or between the individual and the collective, but there is no difference between belief and unbelief, or between believing and unbelieving societies. They deal with the fact that the Christian, although justified, continues to commit sin, and with the further fact that the Christian who bears social responsibility seems to be obligated to do things which Christian love would not call for; they do not in any seriousness take account of the fact that a major proportion of society is made up of people who have not the slightest intention of even attempting Christian idealism, and who feel that it is quite in order that they should use society and even the state as the tools of their selfishness.

The views to which we now turn are distinguished by the fact that they do give consideration to the issue of faith. (The term *sectarian* used to designate this originality is a qualifying epithet which, although it initially had a pejorative sense, is now sometimes used descriptively, as we mean to do here.) This means that we can no longer adequately represent our problem on a single graph, as everyone from the Middle Ages to Reinhold Niebuhr has been trying to do. We must rather have two graphs, one for the ethical realm where faith is a conditioning factor; another for the realm where it is not. It should not be thought that this distinction is a sociological one between two different kinds of groups, as though the assumption were being made that the organized church is the realm of faith and the rest of society the realm of unbelief. The middle line on the graph divides not societies but problem areas.

F. *Jehovah's Witnesses*

In the realm of faith the ethical standard to be applied is not the *agape* of Christ but the law of Old and New Testaments. In

JEHOVAH'S WITNESSES

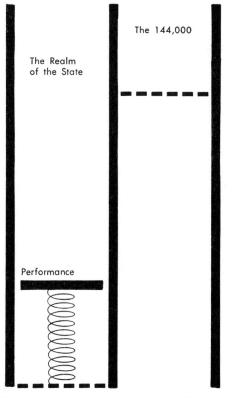

this respect the Jehovah's Witnesses are parallel to the Puritans. This side of the line is not, however, our major concern; we are interested in the norms that can be drawn for the unbelieving society. Since, however, the state in the understanding of the Jehovah's Witnesses is diabolical, there are actually no norms at all to hold up before it.   Jehovah's Witnesses do go to court frequently to claim their rightful liberties, but in doing this they are driven by considerations of publicity and not by a concern for the duties of the state.   If a state does not persecute the faithful it is, in fact, better than its diabolical nature would lead one to expect; it is possible for the performance of the state to exceed in lovingness the essential pattern of the state.   In this situation, it would be pointless to speak regarding any specific duty of the statesman or the institution; the only message is the call to individuals to come and join the multitude of 144,000.

G.   Traditional Amish-Mennonite

The view of the Jehovah's Witnesses was mentioned first in order to distinguish it from other views which also find a difference

AMISH TRADITION

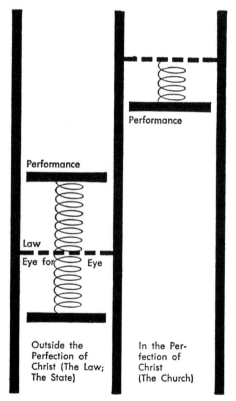

between church and world.   Like the Jehovah's Witnesses, traditional Mennonitism distinguishes between the realm of belief and that of unbelief.   Unlike them, this distinction is not drawn on the narrow basis of denominational affiliation, not claiming that all of the church is in Mennonitism and that all of the world is outside. Unlike the Jehovah's Witnesses, Mennonites and Amish do have standards which they apply to a state to call it to do its duty better. The obvious traditional example is their contesting the legality of religious persecution. At the same time they have recognized the necessity for the state to work on a lower level than that of *agape*. Some have accepted the death penalty as legitimate, and modern conservative Mennonites have made a similar point in their argument against liberal pacifism. This view is thus similar to the Catholic and Lutheran views in that a *distinct* and *definite* level of normative sub-Christian justice is presumed to exist. For him who has made the commitment of faith, nothing stands ultimately in the way of his fully following Christ; similarly, he who would bring about earthly justice could presumably attain it, since its requirements are fixed and known.

There are very obvious differences from the earlier views in defining the standards for Christian behavior. The full New Testament vision of binding (and possible) discipleship norms is maintained for the believer; there is no unrealistic "pacifist" expectation of discipleship performance from the state. Yet as far as what is said about the world is concerned this position is open to the same criticisms as the Roman Catholic and Lutheran views discussed earlier; it posits an independent standard of justice, which is thought to be known somehow apart from Christ. The more conservative representatives of this position would here speak of the Mosaic legislation; contemporary interpreters would sometimes speak of Greco-Roman concepts of fair retribution or of the state's pragmatic obligation to defend its own existence. This independent standard, which can be both known and attained apart from Christ, is challengeable not only because it raises a claim to be revelation outside of Christ but also because it doubts the biblical affirmation that God in Christ is "Lord" over the world.

It was said above that the vertical line dividing the two columns is to be interpreted as signifying only belief as versus unbelief, and not as the institutional distinction between those who are and are not church members or are or are not in the world. If, however, the diversity of standards between the two realms is strongly emphasized, the temptation becomes very strong to "stiffen" the line between the two realms, thinking of the ins and the outs sociologically or even geographically, weakening both the missionary imperative and the relevance of a witness to the state.

H. Proposed New Formulation

The diagram here suggested agrees with the traditional sectarian view in its maintaining the norm of love as the only standard in the

71

church, in maintaining the distinction between the presuppositions of faith and of unfaith, in realistically expecting the standards and the achievement of the world to be less than love, and in considering love to be a relevant historical possibility distinct from self-immolation and from puritan benevolence.

It differs from the traditional sectarian view just as it differs from the medieval positions in challenging the existence or the knowability of a fixed standard of justice in the realm of unbelief. (The theological advantages of this difference have been discussed above in connection with Reinhold Niebuhr.) We therefore avoid affirming that there is any norm willed by God other than love

PROPOSED

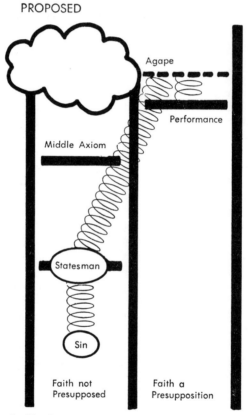

itself. What holds down the performance and the standards that apply in the world is the weight of sin, not a divinely revealed lower order for secular society. God's only ultimate will is what He has revealed in Christ.

The individual citizen or statesman in the world of unbelief cannot see through the wall that separates him from the world of faith. Therefore the point at which the norm of *agape* is understandable and relevant to him is not the top of the scale on his side of the barrier of unbelief. Looking directly up he can see only a cloud, within which he fears there might lie an ideal demand for self-sacrifice, which he understands as suicide, i.e., not a meaningful alternative. The point at which *agape* becomes meaningful for him is rather the point at which the "spring" representing the relevance of love operating from within the realm of faith goes out of his sight through the wall. At this level the norm is formulated for him in pagan terms (liberty, equality, fraternity, education, democracy, human rights). This we have represented by the line *N* for norm, which is not a fixed point but a projection representing the next highest conceivable level of standards to which one can appeal in the world of unbelief.

The point where the "spring" impinges on the line of justice is the individual. He can be appealed to make a leap of faith. This might be a small leap, as far upward as he can see in the direction of the standards that have been held before him; even this clearly requires faith. Or it could be the true leap of faith, taking him beyond the barrier of unbelief to the commitment of discipleship. It will be observed that these norms—or, to use the earlier term, middle axioms—are expressed with no embarrassment in pagan terms, even though it is insisted that the ultimate ground for their validity is the love of Christ; in fact, that they do not even exist except as a reflection or projection of the relevance of that love.

It is therefore possible to explain, or at least to represent graphically, how the Christian can speak to the statesman, without failing to take account of their differing presuppositions, using pagan or secular terminology to clothe his social critique without ascribing to those secular concepts any metaphysical value outside of Christ.

We thus also avoid the confusing possibility that was visible on the other diagrams where the "justice" line was fixed, of having a state actually doing better than it should, such as a state which would be reprimanded by the church for failing to be sufficiently rigorous in the repression of crime or in military preparedness.

8. THEORETICAL UNDERSTANDINGS OF THE STATE

A. Romans 13 and the Institution of the State

IN TRADITIONAL EUROPEAN THEOLOGY much has been made of Romans 13 and similar biblical expressions as indicating that the state has been divinely instituted by a special act of God in creation and/or providence. This has been interpreted in two possible ways. One, which we shall label *positivistic* and which has been represented in the most extreme form in some Lutheran traditions, draws from the conception of the divinely instituted state the conclusion that whatever state now exists in any given time and place is the state which God desires to exist then and there. The Christian shall therefore take the will of the state as being, in its own domain, the will of God. If God providentially places a Bismarck or a Hitler in a position of authority, this reveals the divine intention for that nation, which it is the duty of all Christians to accept and obey believingly. The prince of whom Luther thought in the sixteenth century is replaced today by the professional politician, to whom the simple Christian citizen should in a similar way entrust his political judgment.

The other possible understanding of the divine institution of the state, which we shall call the *legitimistic* and which has received more extended development within the Reformed tradition, would rather say that we can find in Romans 13, or at least in a combination of biblical and rational considerations, certain basic outlines of the prescriptions which God has divinely established for the state to fulfill. The state which fulfills these requirements, or at least sincerely attempts to do so, is legitimate and should be obeyed by the Christian; the state which does not, especially as it consciously sets itself up against the divine standards of justice and humanity, is a non-state, worthy only of destruction. Whether the Christian obeys such a non-state or rebels against it, he may decide on purely pragmatic grounds; he owes it no obedience "for the sake of conscience" and it does not interpret God's will for him.

Whereas the positivistic position was represented during World War II by the so-called German Christians and today is maintained by the Protestant wing of the Adenauer party, especially its most extreme theological spokesman, Professor Künneth, the legitimistic position was represented during the war by Karl Barth and the Confessing Church, and has been driven to the extreme by Bishop Otto Dibelius, who drew the conclusion that, since the Marxist government of East Germany is not committed to Christian moral standards, it is not really a government, and Bishop Dibelius will obey its rules only in order to avoid inconvenience, not because it has any moral authority over him.

These two logical alternatives have been worked out with the greatest clarity and consistency by German thinkers, as is customary, but they represent a problem which is just as troublesome for less thorough analysts. It would seem that these two alternatives are the only available ones, so that we must follow one or the other or some uneasy mixture of the two. Each is obviously unsound when carried to an extreme; when stated soberly each seems to make sense.

The real promise for a solution that would be both logically and biblically proper lies not in the direction of attempting to merge or mix these two views, but in discovering the inadequacy of their starting assumptions. Both agree that Romans 13 affirms that God has established or instituted the state by a specific providential or creative act; then the debate is only about whether he has thus instituted the ideal state or the empirical one.

More careful recent analysis, both exegetical and systematic, has given good reason to doubt whether the intention of Paul in this passage was at all to provide this sort of metaphysic or ontology of the state. Paul was simply arguing that the Christians in Rome should not rebel even against a government which threatened to mistreat them. They could be confident that God was using the powers in and behind the state within His providential purpose. The state is not instituted, i.e., established, but rather accepted in its empirical reality, as something that God can overrule toward His ends. Paul therefore does *not* mean that in the divine acceptance of the state there is implied any ratification of its moral standards or political purposes, or any theory of the proper state.[1]

While differing markedly from the legitimistic view, by finding in Romans 13 instructions to submit to *any* state, this understanding differs as well from the positivistic view by denying that the acceptance of the state by God means any divine endorsement of its moral judgments or practical purposes. The Christian is called not to *obey* the state, which would imply actually receiving from the state his moral guidance, but to *be subject*, which means simply that he shall not rebel or seek to act as if the state were not there. Whether he obeys the state or finds that his submission must be in the form of disobedience and accepting punishment for it, will depend on what the state asks of him.[2]

1 The NEB follows the traditional "institutional" view by expanding the Greek "under God" into "by act of God." Paul is not affirming any specific divine action establishing any particular Roman, Parthian, or Scythian government (as there were acts of God creating Israel); he is saying that whatever agency is ruling, it is within the divine ordering.
2 C.E.B. Cranfield has made abundantly clear that Paul is here writing about something quite distinct from *obedience*. *New Testament Studies*, *VI* (1960) fascicle 3 (April), pp. 241 ff., "Some Observations on Romans 13:1-7."

B. The Two Faces of the State in the New Testament

A frequently used pattern of exposition sees Romans 13 with the exhortation to be subject to the state as an ordinance of God, as counterbalanced by Revelation 13 with its vision of the diabolical beast from the abyss. Some argue that this proves the inconsistency of the early church's attitude toward the state. Others, however,[3] more numerous and more serious, would argue that the state can in any age exist in one of two forms. It can on the one hand be a sober and righteous instrument of order in society, in which case the duty of the Christian is submission enjoined in Romans 13. On the other hand, there is the possibility that a state may become directly rebellious against the law of God, as symbolically expressed in the beast of the apocalypse, the responsibility of a church at that point being that presumedly to deny its authority or right to exist.

As illuminating as this analysis at first appears, with its desire to understand the New Testament witness as internally consistent, and with the willingness to make a clear negative judgment at some points, a number of other considerations stand in the way of our accepting it. As is the case with a somewhat broader idea that the state may not take on "religious" claims,[4] it is hard to see just what objective criterion would furnish the means of knowing definitely when a given state moves from one category into the other.

A further caution is due at this point because Revelation 13 is not directly concerned with the state. Clearly, the "beast" is a political figure; the total concern of the passage, the meaning of the vision, is, however, not a discussion of what it is that makes a state an unjust state, but rather of the unfaithfulness of spokesmen of the *church* who relate to the state in an idolatrous and unfaithful way; the subject of Revelation 13 is apostasy and not politics.

The traditional legitimistic approach would grasp upon this distinction between Romans 13 and Revelation 13, as illustrating the point at which a state, once recognized as unjust, should no longer be respected by Christians, who should rather aid the forces of rebellion. For this interpretation there is no biblical warrant. The task of Christians in Revelation 13 is not to rebel in any politically relevant way; it is suffering submission, "the patience and faithfulness of the saints."

We should then better say that Romans 13 and Revelation 13

---

3 One well-known text playing Romans 13 and Revelations 13 against one another as two alternative possibilities is Karl Barth's (W. Herberg, *op. cit.*, 114 ff.). "The question . . . which the state cannot evade is, Does it make clear or obscure the significance of the political order as service of God? Is it on the way to becoming in its sphere what Romans 13 calls God's representative and priest or is it on the way to becoming the beast rising up out of the sea of Revelation 13? *It is either one or the other.*"—Karl Barth, *The Knowledge of God and the Service of God.* Hodder and Stoughton, 3d. ed. 1955, p. 226 (our italics).

4 Cf. pp. 33 f. above.

represent the two dimensions of the life of any state. In any state we can see self-glorification and the combining of religious and political motivations. The wielding of the sword is always an expression of a degree of unbelief, and the church that blesses this undertaking is always marked by a measure of apostasy. Yet, on the other hand, every state as well is, in the words of Romans 13, "under God," with its justice and its injustices equally integrated within God's universal redemptive plan. No state can be so low on the scale of relative justice that the duty of the Christian is no longer to be subject; no state can rise so high on that scale that Christians are not called to some sort of suffering because of their refusal to agree with its self-glorification and the resultant injustices.

C. The State "as Such"

It may be critically noted that while speaking of the witness that the Christian can render to the state we have not chosen one of the available theories of just what the state is and should be. The witness rendered to the bearers of power, we have claimed, is motivated in our love for them as men and for their subjects and is rooted in the very meaning of the gospel which we proclaim as it includes the social realm in its promises of renewal and its message of judgment; we have founded this witness in the centrality of the church and the instrumental relationship of the political order to the church's work; we have founded it in rejection of idolatry. In other words, the witness to the state has never been *based on* a theory about what the state is and should be in itself, nor has it been rendered *for the sake of* the state "in itself."

What we have just said of the reason for speaking to the state applies also to what we say of how the state should operate. The claims we lay on statesmen are not founded in any particular theory. We would call for an increasing degree of democratization, without believing in any way that the voice of the majority is infallible or that the state reposes on the foundation of a social contract. We can call on the state to respect its own constitution without assuming that constitution to be better than another. We can call statesmen to respect certain constant values in the realms of family, work, and school without believing that nature or creation is discernibly and rigidly structured in a limited number of "orders" constituting intrinsic obligations for all men.

Most traditional approaches to the state, including those referred to above in our survey of the classical understanding of Romans 13, have proceeded deductively from a general theory of what the state is and should be to the specific instructions directed to men of state. This approach assumes that the most valid truths are the most general ones, and that the process of reasoning from the general to the particular is the most reliable way to deepen one's understanding of truth and its application. Christians using this approach furthermore tend to assume that it is in the form of generalizations that revelation about the state is given, or that the relevance of any particular statements or examples from history must pass over the bridge of broad generalities.

But, though itself questionable, this deductive procedure is not the most dubious characteristic of the theories of the state which operate in this way. Still more challengeable are some further presuppositions inherent in this approach. One is seen in the test question, What would happen if this Christian approach were carried to the extreme?[5] Where would it lead if what we ask of Christians were done by everyone, and carried to the nth degree?

This is an application of the criterion of generalizability in ethics, by virtue of which it is assumed that a moral judgment is only valid if it can be applied to all men without restriction. We have noted elsewhere that this assumption, axiomatic as it has become in our civilization, is nonetheless fundamentally unbiblical; for it forgets that Christian moral judgments are related to regeneration, to forgiveness, to the church, and to the Christian hope in such a way that they cannot have the same relevance outside the circle of faith. That the state might listen to the Christian message and obey it to the point of ceasing to exist is by definition impossible; the fear of such an outcome may never justify neglecting the proclamation of any element of the divine demand.

A further shortcoming of the approach which begins first with a theory of the state is its inherent incapacity to make a clear distinction between what is and what should be. The more clear the definition of the theoretical state, the less it will describe or speak relevantly to any actually functioning state; the logical conclusion to draw is that there is always at least a degree of rebellion, as is

5 Gordon Clark, writing in *Christianity Today* (Vol. IV, No. 9, Feb. 1, 1960, p. 354) argues, "Until the opponents of capital punishment formulate their theory of civil authority, nothing more need be said. . . ." Professor Clark, an utterly consistent philosopher, assumes that one can begin with a theory of government, derived from biblical or other sources, and that such a theory must explain both the existence of government and the grounds of our specific criticism of it or suggestions to it as well as in extreme cases our possible rebellion against it. It is assumed that if one does not have a theory justifying the existence of government one has no grounds for criticizing governmental performance.

We must respect the logical coherence of Clark's presuppositions; they are, however, logical presuppositions and not biblical affirmations. The state does not need to be theoretically justified in order to exist; it does exist. Whether our speaking to the state presupposes that we must have a theory of why the state exists will depend on the nature and ground of our critique. For Calvin and for Clark both the state's existence and the instructions they would address to it are based in the same theocratic ideal; but Clark has no logical right to require of other positions that they share this axiom. His challenging the possibility of any other kind of social critique by this *reductio ad absurdum* is thus not a substantive argument but a philosophic confession of faith. Paul's acceptance of Roman rule makes no use of the idea, central to Clark, that standards for any state can be read out of Genesis.

always implied in the legitimistic view; and thus no state is biblically ever fully authorized. The other logical possibility is to save the theory by keeping it so extremely permissive and vague as to render any precise critique impossible.

D. That "Other Realm"

Behind our discussions of Romans 13 and the effort to summarize graphically the varieties of approach to our problem there lies a recurrent theme which we are now ready to approach more directly. For some this theme can be adequately labeled with terms such as *natural law,* or more broadly, *natural theology;* many, however, who would reject these terms still maintain under some other heading the pattern of thought which we seek here to identify as "that other realm" and to evaluate theologically.

Common to these varied lines of thought is the idea that somewhere between outright sin on the one hand and the will of God as revealed in Jesus Christ and His cross on the other, there lies an additional fixed point or points to which we must also ascribe the quality of moral bindingness, whether we speak of this authority as being rooted in revelation or not. In the sketches above, this understanding has generally been represented by a fixed line which we labeled "justice." In the case, however, of Reinhold Niebuhr, for whom justice is not a *fixed* point, it remains nonetheless fully clear that it is in any situation an identifiable value, morally binding upon men, and not identical with *agape.*

H. Richard Niebuhr has sought to ground this moral axiom more theologically by giving it a trinitarian frame. Insofar as the "other standards" are conceived of as grounded in creation, he attributes them to God the Father; insofar as they represent historically the experience of the Christian community, he would identify them with the Spirit.[6] The most widespread traditional way of speaking of this realm is as we have indicated above in the discussion of natural law; it is claimed that there is written into "nature"—either that of the universal society or that of specific persons and organizations—an understanding of or capacity for a certain type or level of moral insight or performance, which itself constitutes the ground of the knowability and the bindingness of moral norms. Those theologians who in the tradition of Karl Barth reject the idea of natural law still tend to retain some conception of "the state as such" or of the "legal state" which retains in effect more of this pattern of thought than they tend to want to

---

6 This "trinitarian" analysis, a major theme of the argument of *Christ and Culture* (Harper, 1951, esp. pp. 80 f., 114, 131), was already sketched in the late Prof. Niebuhr's earlier article "The Doctrine of the Trinity and the Unity of the Christ," *Theology Today,* October 1946, pp. 371 ff. The three persons of the Godhead represent not only distinguishable *sources* of Christian insight; they may also provide contradictory *imperatives.*

admit. We see this most clearly when such thinkers assume that it is possible to identify quite accurately the specific point at which a state would move from sobriety into idolatry; i.e., the point at which a state would be taking on religious claims.

What is it that all of the thinkers cited above have in common, in spite of their great variety, which enables us at this point to group them all in the treatment of one basic issue?

a) In all of these positions it is understood that there is an ethical standard distinct from Jesus Christ in that it requires of man action not immediately reconcilable with the teaching and example of Jesus. All of these positions claim that "other level" of moral obligation is not simply an arbitrary midpoint on the scale between complete obedience and complete rebellion, but that it is identifiable, and knowable, apart from Christ. Whether we refer to this realm as "moral philosophy" in distinction from "moral theology," as does traditional Roman Catholicism, as the "orders of creation" with Lutheranism or with Emil Brunner, as the "mandates" with Dietrich Bonhoeffer, as "Greco-Roman concepts of justice" with Reinhold Niebuhr, or as a natural law, is here immaterial. Common to all is the tacit or explicit claim that this other standard of "justice" 1) is knowable apart from Jesus Christ and 2) differs from Him in what it demands of men.

b) These standards are not only knowable and distinguishable from Jesus Christ; they are also morally binding. At least for most men (with the exception of the clergy in Catholic thought), or for most realms of human behavior (with the exception of the purely individual relationships in the thought of Martin Luther or Reinhold Niebuhr), the claims which these standards of justice lay upon man are *prior* to those derived from the love of Christ. This love, to use a now classical phrasing of Reinhold Niebuhr, can remain a principle of criticism, both of "indiscriminate criticism" in that it drives all men to repentance, and of "discriminate criticism" in that it demands creative dissatisfaction with past and present compromises; but the love of Christ *should not* actually dictate our behavior, for what this world needs, at least in most realms and from most men, is justice. Reinhold Niebuhr has only drawn out with great rigor and honesty what is implicit in most other views.

c) Not only is this "lower level" of justice actually the fundamental obligation which an individual should take upon himself within the social order; it is also of such moral bindingness that it is the business of the statesman—and every Christian should somehow be a statesman—to impose it, by force if necessary in extreme cases, upon the recalcitrant neighbor.

The criticism which we must address to all of these positions in common is a twofold one. Either of the aspects of this criticism should suffice, in fact, to render questionable the common features of all these approaches; yet there would be something missing if both lines of the criticism did not coincide.

The first fundamental criticism, which can be stated the more simply and (in the proper sense of this term) dogmatically, is that the honest Christian thinker must encounter with a great suspicion, if not automatic rejection, any central ideas which come to him claiming to have revelatory authority apart from and, in fact, over against Jesus Christ. It is, especially since the analysis of Reinhold Niebuhr, incontrovertibly clear that that is what such positions all do. They claim that within the realm of the state's responsibility there are insights or understandings or principles or ways of working at problems which have the same kind of authority over men including Christians, that Christ himself claims, yet which calls men to do things that Christ (as we know Him from the New Testament) does not call men to do.

It is no answer to this objection to argue, as it is, of course, possible to do, that it is also Christ who is the foundation of the knowability or the bindingness of other standards, but that in these realms Christ is the eternal *Logos* operative in creation and history, or that Jesus himself enjoins us to love our neighbors, which means seeking the neighbors' welfare, which in turn means concern for justice. These claims are ancient and respectable theological options, which we want to understand with great seriousness as we question them, but they do not refute the descriptive statement made above that they set up other norms against the Christ of the New Testament. In this usage such terms as "love of neighbor" or "the eternal Christ operative in creation and history" are simply paraphrases of this competitive revelational claim.

The second, less dogmatic and perhaps for some the more convincing argument against the revelation claim of this "other realm" of justice, is the internal critique which flows from an analysis of the efforts made to take such a position seriously. The great diversity of the positions listed above, all of them sharing this option, itself testifies that it is much more convincing when they use it as an argument against simple discipleship than when they face the challenge of spelling out in detail what justice actually means.[7]

One of the classical expressions of this unclarity is the ambiguity with which Martin Luther dealt with the state. On the one hand, by considering the state as an extension of the order of the family, he could call it a "good creation" and understand it as a result not of the Fall, but of the divine creative intention for order within the

7 Cf. above pp. 30 f.

pre-Fall creation. Yet at the same time it is the duty of the state to wield the sword; something for which the world before the Fall had no place. If the use of the sword were understood as somehow an undesirable or regrettable accretion to the real function of the state, this could be understood; but both Catholic and Protestant doctrine have always argued that the sword is part of the essence of the state. By thus merging two intrinsically contradictory understandings of the state, Martin Luther gave to government a degree of divine sanction independent both of Christ and of justice which has been a problem to Protestantism ever since.

But Luther should not be considered particularly blameworthy as some sought to do in Hitler's time, but simply as extremely typical. Everyone who has sought to describe the order which he felt clearly to be revealed in nature has concluded by projecting his own understanding of the world's needs; the meanings of *nature* have been as varied as the histories of men who have tried to define what would be *natural.*" The "law of nature" has been evoked in favor of both democracy and the divine right of kings, both primitive communism and capitalistic free enterprise. All that these various positions have in common is that they claim it is possible to set up over against the incarnation another set of norms; but when we come to asking what these norms might be, we find we have learned nothing from the statement that they are in nature.[8] *Nature* may be the struggle of the species for survival; it may be the existing social order in its interplay of hierarchies and power claims; or, on the other hand, it may be the *essence* of a person or thing that he is called to become. The word thus includes two different scales of variability; when *nature* is understood to mean a quasi-platonic *essence,* distinct from what things appear to do, we have the whole gamut of *ideals* which have not yet been actualized in experience; if, on the other hand by *nature* we understand "things as they are," we must deal with the entire scale of empirical realities. The conviction, almost universally shared, that nature is a reliable source of knowable and binding ethical norms rests on failure to clarify either the content which it claims to have proved or the truth claims which it presupposes.[9]

8 Donald Miller has argued for a new definition of "natural law" as still both desirable and adequate ("Does Natural Law Provide a Basis For a Christian Witness to the State? *Brethren Life and Thought,* Spring 1962, Vol. VII, No. 2, pp. 8 ff; cf. our Rejoinder in the same issue). Miller saves the term *natural law* only by giving it still another meaning, neither natural nor law.

9 Jacques Ellul, "Concerning the Christian Attitude Toward Law," *Christian Scholar,* Vol. XLII, No. 2, 1959, pp. 139 ff., and *Le Fondement Theologique du Droit,* Neuchatel/ Paris, 1946, is the most persuasive advocate of the view advocated here, that the only "metaphysical" ground for the complex of ideas and institutions which we call *justice* is the fact of their presence; that we do wrong to base them in anything else thought to be more broadly valid, whether in reason, in the nature of man or society, or in some special divine creative act. To advocates of the view that justice as a distinct value is "written in the human heart" or enshrined by God in nature or society, the "positivistic" position taken here seems philosophically irresponsible.

The widespread distinction between two sources of obligation springs not so much from any *a priori* self-evident duality in the way knowledge actually reaches us as from an effort to understand apparently conflicting moral demands. We should therefore not expect to be able to pursue the examination of this problem further in the abstract; we must ask about the origin and the justification of specific claims, such as the argument that there must be a certain amount of violence or of retribution in the social order. This should confirm the wisdom of our dealing first with sample moral issues rather than with a theoretical grasp of the state.

How could we conceivably go about testing these two claims against one another? At what point would it make any difference whether justice as distinct both from love and from the factuality of sin is a divine institution in its own right? It would seem that the only conceivable testing process would be to imagine the most hypothetical case of a pre-Fall society where there is no sinful self-affirmation, then to ask whether in such a situation there would need to be violence or retribution. That there would need to be some kind of order is not debatable; but would this order need to express itself in either violence or vengeance? Since in this hypothetical paradise there would be first of all no intentional offenses and secondly no one selfishly demanding vengeance, the claims for the need for retributive justice are hard to conceive of. Likewise distributive justice in such a context would mean giving everyone his share, which everyone in Eden would accept as sufficient. Could *agape* mean more than this? If *agape* be defined as different from justice, in such a situation it could only mean giving up one's own share, not because of someone else's greater need but for the sake of suffering and sacrifice as ends in themselves. This, however, would be Hindu self-abnegation, not Christian self-sacrifice. Thus, a situation where Christian *agape* would be different from justice cannot be conceived of apart from the Fall. We therefore stand by the claim that the only basis for justice, either as an idea or as a set of institutions, is the fallenness of men individually and socially. We can, of course, continue to conceive of natural law in the scientific sense of observed repeatability; but then the claim can no longer be upheld that justice in natural law is a moral norm competing for our loyalty with that of *agape*.

9. MISUSE OF THE CHURCH/WORLD DICHOTOMY

A. The Bogey of Pietism

THE CONCERN OF THE PRESENT study coincides at numerous points, yet with meaningful differences, with studies of the Christian foundation of social ethics stimulated in recent years by the Division of Studies of the World Council of Churches as well as by its precursor in the same field of concern, the World Student Christian Federation. Focusing on the slogan "responsible society" between Amsterdam 1948 and Evanston 1954, looking with equal concentration at the problems of younger nations and younger churches in the "Rapid Social Change" studies between Evanston and New Delhi 1961, these ecumenical efforts have gathered expert counsel on numerous problems of social ethics and carried a concern for the Christian witness to the social order into every corner of the world church. For this we are grateful; the present comment has to do not with the intent but with the mode of this undertaking.

A constantly recurrent theme in ecumenical writings[1] is the sharp and steady critique addressed to what they call "pietism." Without resorting to laborious citation, the meaning of the term as here used can be summarized as follows:

Both in Western churches and in their missions there has been a current of thought which held that the church should not be concerned for social ethics. The difference between Christians and non-Christians was strongly drawn, largely in terms of individual ethics, especially negatively with relation to alcohol, tobacco, and the dance. Beyond this there was not only a very limited awareness of the moral dimensions of broader social phenomena, but in fact a definite conviction that Christians should be little concerned with them.

M. M. Thomas sets pietism in apposition to "withdrawal from the world of social structures and power politics." The Student Christian Movement, growing from an individualistic missionary motivation to an awareness of the social implications of both unbelief and the gospel, had to break through the bonds of this pietist tradition, and although few live pietists are active within the World Council leadership, the dialogue with this hypothetic adversary of all Christian social critique remains one of the most graphic and most frequent ways of making points in discussions of social ethics.

---

1 Pierre Maury, *Politics and Evangelism,* Association, 1959, especially pp. 45 ff.; M. M. Thomas, in *Ecumenical Review,* January 1962, p. 250 f. heads a paragraph, "Fighting the Tradition of Pietism." These writings are singled out because they are recent and because their authors are accredited spokesmen of the ecumenical movement; their number could be multiplied.

What we here question is not the Christian social concern itself, but the aptness of the reference to pietism as a description of the issues at stake. The problem in understanding past inadequacies of Christian social responsibility is more than one of mere words; behind words ineptly used there may hide errors of diagnosis and then perhaps also of therapy.

Pietism was a specific movement in church history. Contemporary use of the term raises first of all the question of the relation between the reproaches being expressed and that historical movement. Every contemporary option assumes a view of history; if the history is misread the light it throws on the present may also be colored.

It is certainly not the case that pietism, whether we think now of the eighteenth century movement or of its more recent spiritual heirs, was uninterested in social or political ethics. Few movements in church history and few schools of theological conviction have been, in proportion to population, so productive of institutional inventiveness and cultural creativity as have been the Moravians, the Methodists, and their counterparts within the larger churches. Obviously, they met the social issues of their age and not ours. They opened schools, freed slaves, reduced languages to writing, and trained nurses rather than writing constitutions, negotiating test bans, and training economists. We are not called to imitate the pietists; but we confuse and impoverish ourselves if we think to identify our current concerns by disavowing their example. In their times, in terms of options then available, their response to the social-ethical issues then visible was the creative and original one.

Secondly, pietism, whether in the time of Francke or today in the Fundamentalism derived partly from it, has always had a definite political philosophy and acted in accordance with it. The nobility, practicing politicians, and military men have always figured prominently in pietist circles. Whether "at home" in the Christian West or abroad in "foreign missions," the specialized minister or missionary avoided political involvement *not* because such involvement was not the Christian's business, but because someone else *from his church* was exercising that calling within the division of labor which his views of both society and the church called for. When pietists raised the cry, "Keep the church out of politics," it was not out of the conviction that politics is not a field for Christians, but rather because the Christians who considered themselves called to politics as their vocation resented the interference and the critiques of churchmen.

If, therefore, there was something wrong with the political ethics of pietism, it must have been in the *how* and not the *whether*. If there was error, it was not that of abstention but the wrong kind of

85

involvement. But then the conversation today, if it is to move beyond jousting with absent adversaries, must also touch the *how*, not the *whether*. With this shift suddenly the predominant themes in recent ecumenical study seem less original; in fact, certain striking agreements with pietism come to light.

1. Pietism has generally proceeded from a fundamentally positive response to the given political-historical situation; this positive evaluation was derived both from a strong sense of Providence and an equally strong confidence in the Christian's capacity to discern the meaning of current events. In the age of the divine right of kings pietism was not democratic; in Anglo-Saxon democracy it has not been royalist; in Hitler's Germany it was not strongly represented in the Confessing Church. When in a revolutionary age Christians see in the rise of young nations the hand of God[2] or when east of the iron curtain today certain theologians illuminate not only their own history but also that of the rest of the world in the light of 1917[3] we again have to do with essentially the same posture; with the discernment in a given stream of history (noteworthily not that of the visible church alone) of that institution in which the hand of God is to be welcomed. We are not here concerned with labeling such positions as right or wrong, but with recognizing their place within the pietistic tradition.

2. Pietism has tended to assume that social leadership is the business of the state, which solves problems by creating and changing institutions. If slavery is wrong it should be outlawed; if the heathen in dark Africa are to be helped the King must charter a society; if our soldiers are to hear the gospel there must be a uniformed chaplaincy. Pietists tended not only to respect political authorities in the powers they had, but also to propose to them new functions as the most obvious way to meet new needs. This same confidence in the state as the obvious means of helpfully structuring society is shared by many contemporary ecumenical thinkers.[4] The church's peculiar functions—as an exemplary society living on a level of fellowship and service unattainable by the state, as guardian of humanitarian impulses and concern for the individual, as bridge

2 M. M. Thomas, writing about 1950 in *Christians in the Contemporary World Struggle,* WSCF Geneva (no date), pp. 4-40, spoke of world revolution in such a hopeful tone that his critics Chevallier and Bridston (ibid. pp. 93 ff., 119 ff.) seem much less "western" than he.

3 A tendency, or at least a temptation, in some of the writings of Prof. Josef Hromadka.

4 A working paper prepared with great care and representativity under the auspices of the Commission on Ecumenical Mission and Relations of the United Presbyterian Church in the U.S.A. places "service in the political sphere" in top place under the heading "Priorities in Service." In the same communities where generations ago Methodist preachers forbade liquor sales by law because it was easier than winning their members to voluntary abstinence, ministers today call on city or state authorities to forbid racial discrimination in real estate sales, while most of the sellers and real estate agents are members of their church. Franklin H. Littell's comment on this was cited above, Chap. 3, Note 5.

between nations, races, and classes, as inventor of kinds of service for which the state does not sense the need—continue to be alluded to in the preambles to ecumenical documents; yet the bulk of the discussion centers in how the entire society should be governed by the state and how the church contributes to this process by sending consecrated individuals into public service (i.e., state employment) and by speaking to major moral issues. A major reason for this reliance on the state is, of course, the desire that whatever solution one finds to a social problem, it must be binding for all. Christians desirous of overcoming the ghetto mentality are not inclined to accept standards which set them apart from their neighbors; moral ideals applying only to Christians, incapable of changing a whole society effectively, are by that very characteristic disqualified.

3. The minister of the gospel himself, or the church as institution charged with the administration of preaching and the sacraments, should according to pietism only very rarely speak directly to political issues. This could happen most easily when it came to identifying certain sins which the state should repress; otherwise the church (i.e., the clergy) should avoid partisan postures in the daily debate about problems "where there is no clear right and wrong."[5] This tendency remains alive in ecumenical circles; the layman whose business it is should be effective in politics, but the preachers and the church should not except in extreme situations. This leads to most characteristic results in countries ruled by the multi-party system, where the advice is given to Christians in the exercise of their social responsibility to join not one party but all of them. Thus, whenever the votes are counted Christians will have voted, each in the name of social responsibility laid on him by the gospel, on both sides, largely canceling out each other's responsibility and reproducing within their impact on society roughly the same scattering of votes as obtains in the larger society, i.e., having a conservative and not a critical impact, which is precisely the pietist pattern.

The dangers of clericalism and of whitewashing all too human causes by the appeal to religious sanctions are clear; it is self-evident what the advocates of pluralism in Christian social responsibility are trying to avoid. But, when to avoid this evil the idea that Christians should be on the same side on any significant social issue is abandoned even as a hypothetical goal, and the whether of involvement is placed above the how, the result is the opposite of that intended.

4. The standards of pietist social involvement were drawn from

5 Any careful critic will have noticed that the phrase quoted is petitionary; we are discussing precisely what is right and wrong. Its equivalent can be found all the way back to the Augsburg Confession Art. XVI; it shows the legalistic and uncritical mood of thought often resorted to in the effort to exempt daily moral decisions from binding Christian criticism.

that broad realm of intelligent insights and observable tendencies usually lumped under the heading "natural law." This is just as true for the traditional cultural options (alcohol, tobacco, the dance, the Mother Hubbard) as for social goals. The theological foundation of such goals, apart from proof texts applied a posteriori, was usually a broad kind of humanism and a hopeful view of providence rather than any deep understanding of the nature of evil, of the state, of institutions, or of the church. This reliance on natural law is again typical of recent ecumenical thought.[6] Only by resorting to natural law, it is felt, can laymen of differing origins get on with the job of social ethics without waiting for the theologians of differing schools to agree on whether and why it is proper for them to do so.[7] The main orientation point in natural law ethics is the concept of "office" or "station"; wherever a man stands in society is spoken of as "where God has placed you" and that station itself defines his duties. Few themes have been more frequent in ecumenical thought in recent years than the "rediscovery of vocation," which usually means not so much judging the mores and obligations of one's profession by the gospel as believing that one's profession is the way to serve one's fellows.

Other lines could be drawn between pietism and ecumenical thought,[8] but such an enterprise is not in our interest. Further analysis would only reaffirm that both where we agree with current ecumenical emphasis in social ethics[9] and where we differ[10] the same similarities obtain. An adolescent is never so clearly his father's child as in the way he chooses to prove his independence.

B. The Strategy of Withdrawal

Another kind of otherworldliness, logically and historically distinct from that of the pietists, has been that of religio-ethnic

6 Papers by Charles C. West and John H. Yoder on the history and meaning of the ecumenical slogan "responsible society" are available from the Secretariat of the Puidoux Theological Conference, Eysseneckstrasse 54, Frankfurt am Main, Germany.

7 At least one ecumenical document on social ethics was written by the simple process of sending the theologian members of the commission into another room to write the preamble while the laymen wrote the body of the report. The laymen in question were, of course, recognized leaders in their professions, i.e., the modern equivalent of the nobles whom pietism expected to fulfill the function of elite leadership, and their ethical insights must have been illuminated substantially by their professional experience.

8 The historical rootage in the Y.M.C.A. and the student Christian movements; the avoidance of the problem of structure which means that an essentially occasionalistic and congregationalist movement ends by favoring connectionalism and revitalizing older structures.

9 The centrality of missionary witness, fellowship, and service as versus the traditional tests of orthodoxy; the special concerns of the department of the laity, the biblical and christological orientation of interchurch conversation.

10 The preoccupation with an ethic for every man, the self-consciousness about the odor of the "ghetto" (which meant, historically, not the enclave chosen by a self-righteous group but that refuge into which society drove those whose loyalty to the God of Abraham made them cosmopolitans and therefore misfits within the religiously colored Volkstum of medieval Europe); confidence in the state, identification of the power elite with the moral elite, natural law.

minority groups like the Mennonites, whose cultural apartness seems both to dramatize and to facilitate their political nonconformity. Since John C. Bennett gave currency to the phrase *strategy of withdrawal*[11] it has been accepted by some conservative Mennonites as a fair statement of their intention.[12] Contemporary analysis is thus marked by a striking series of agreements between the Niebuhrian and the Mennonite positions:[13]

—that Jesus taught and practiced nonresistance (as against the traditional Protestant arguments about the centurion in Capernaum, the cleansing of the temple, and the two swords in the upper room);

—that government, including the use of the sword, and even possible resort to war, is here to stay (as against utopian or anarchistic pacifism);

—that the other position is the only honest and logical alternative to one's own; *tertium non datur.*

This is not the place to argue why these apparent agreements must be denounced as misleading; this argument, and the mandate for a position different from both, not a mere inconsistent mixture of both but recognizing additional dimensions, has been the subject of the entire pamphlet. Here we limit ourselves to an effort to understand the basis of this so widely shared misconception.

1. This misunderstanding was easily accepted because of a lack of ecumenical earnestness. For traditional Mennonites, the responsible position is divinely ordained; there must be such people in society, but true Christians should not be in offices where the use of the sword is unavoidable. To grant to the Niebuhrian that his position is logically consistent means that the Mennonite writes off the other's Christian confession as, if not insincere, at least irrelevant for their continuing relations, for the Niebuhrian has opted to behave in a way that is logical only for pagans. Similarly, while the Niebuhrians recognize the Mennonites as consistent, it is the consistency of error. Their rejection of public responsibility is itself the denial of the most indispensable social meaning of Christian love, and their refusal to be content with vocational recognition as gadflies, who are tolerable on condition that they don't claim to

11 John C. Bennett, *Christian Ethics and Social Policy*, New York, 1946, pp. 41 ff. Bennett used the term to describe Guy F. Hershberger's *War, Peace and Nonresistance* (Scottdale). Hershberger had, however, not used the term and in the revised edition of *War, Peace and Nonresistance* (1953) 230 ff. contested its appropriateness.

12 Example: Statement of the Evangelical Mennonite Conference in *Canadian Mennonite*, July 12, 1963. This writer's own use of the phrase in *Concern 1* was in another context and did not have the implication discussed here, but it did lend itself to misunderstanding in this direction.

13 These labels refer to ideal types and not to persons. The "Niebuhrians" include such a friend of the believers' church vision as Franklin H. Littell (cf. Chap. 1, Note 2) and even some Mennonites; the "Mennonite" attitude is a logical type as defined within the framework the present paper challenges.

be right, is pride, the worst kind of sin. Each party can compliment the other's consistency as a paradigm of the position one rejects, but at the price of no longer owing one another the duties of mutual recognition and admonition which obtain among Christian brethren.

2. The misunderstanding was favored by a falsely selective historiography. Mennonite history is a series of emigrations, of cultural, political, and geographical withdrawals. One of the motives of some of these moves has been to avoid military service obligations. What could be more logical than to read the history as an interpretation of the logic of nonresistance and the trek to the frontier as a search for places where life would be kept simple by the paucity of neighbors and nonresistance kept possible by non-involvement in social duties? But the history does not live up to the logic. Most Mennonites did not migrate. Of those who did, most were not fleeing conscription; and even when they were, the motivation was never a nonresistant logic, scrupulously deducing consequences from the refusal of arms.[14] The refusal to bear arms was itself too traditionally and legalistically motivated for that. Migration to the frontiers, far from being the fruit of a scrupulous respect for the logic of discipleship, was motivated primarily by the desire to survive; first, in evading real persecution, and later, less defensibly, to maintain ethnic and cultural patterns (unrelated to nonresistance) which freer social intercourse would challenge.

3. The misunderstanding was encouraged by a culturally conditioned feeling of inferiority. As for the first time American Mennonites actively entered the broader intellectual life of modern America, the hunger for some kind of acceptance was deep. The conditioned recognition of the Niebuhrians was still more benevolent than any hearing Mennonite convictions had found from other main-line Protestants; it seemed better to be honored by being written off as consistent prophets and pharisees than not to be noticed at all.

4. To this psychological defensiveness was joined an intellectual subservience. It is normal for the newcomer to a debate which is already in process to accept the prevailing definitions of terms and choose one of the existing sides, whereas the wiser approach is to question the definitions. Thus, often the Niebuhrian identification of culture with politics and of social responsibility with the sword is swallowed whole, and then a heroic effort is made to advocate a position whose very definition was framed with a view to making it untenable.

14 Quakers stepped out of the government of Pennsylvania in revolutionary times not because their pacifism disqualified them to support a war effort they nonetheless believed in, but because the individual Quakers in power were no longer Quaker enough in understanding or commitment to be able to continue to make any case for minority rule.